The
BEST of
EXPERTS

Dr. D. G. Hessayon

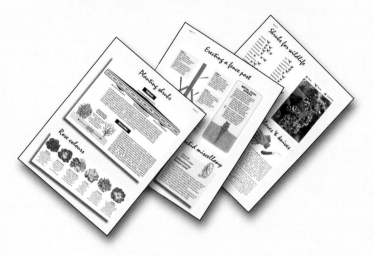

Published by Expert Books
a division of Transworld Publishers

Copyright © Dr. D. G. Hessayon 2010

The right of Dr. D. G. Hessayon to be identified
as author of this work has been asserted in accordance with sections
77 and 78 of the Copyright Designs and Patents Act 1988.

A catalogue record for this book is available from the British Library

TRANSWORLD PUBLISHERS
61-63 Uxbridge Road, London W5 5SA
a division of the Random House Group Ltd

EXPERT BOOKS

Reproduction by Spot On Digital Imaging Ltd, Gomm Road, High Wycombe, Bucks HP13 7DJ
Printed and bound by Butler Tanner & Dennis Ltd, Frome & London

ISBN 978 0 903505 93 2

Introduction

Over the past 50 years the Experts have dominated the gardening book world. Many millions of readers in Britain and overseas have turned to them for instruction, identification, plant history or just an armchair read in winter.

In the following pages you will find some of the favourite items chosen by the author from all the titles, ranging from the very first one to the Expert which he wrote half a century later.

The **BEDDING PLANT EXPERT**
Dr. D. G. Hessayon
THE WORLD'S BEST-SELLING BOOK ON BEDDING PLANTS

The **BEST of EXPERTS**
Dr. D. G. Hessayon
A selection by the author from all the gardening Experts

The **BULB EXPERT**
Dr. D. G. Hessayon
THE WORLD'S BEST-SELLING BOOK ON BULBS

The **CONTAINER EXPERT**
Dr. D. G. Hessayon
THE WORLD'S BEST-SELLING BOOK ON CONTAINER GARDENING

The **EASY-CARE GARDENING EXPERT**
Dr. D. G. Hessayon
THE WORLD'S BEST-SELLING BOOK ON EASY-CARE GARDENING

The **EVERGREEN EXPERT**
Dr. D. G. Hessayon
THE WORLD'S BEST-SELLING BOOK ON EVERGREENS

The **FLOWER EXPERT**
Dr. D. G. Hessayon
THE WORLD'S BEST-SELLING BOOK ON FLOWERS

The **FLOWER ARRANGING EXPERT**
Dr. D. G. Hessayon
THE WORLD'S BEST-SELLING BOOK ON FLOWER ARRANGING

The **FLOWERING SHRUB EXPERT**
Dr. D. G. Hessayon
THE WORLD'S BEST-SELLING BOOK ON FLOWERING SHRUBS

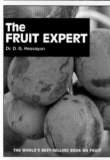
The **FRUIT EXPERT**
Dr. D. G. Hessayon
THE WORLD'S BEST-SELLING BOOK ON FRUIT

The **GREEN GARDEN EXPERT**
Dr. D. G. Hessayon
A NEW VERSION OF THE WORLD'S BEST-SELLER WITH THE ENVIRONMENT IN MIND

The **GARDEN DIY EXPERT**
Dr. D. G. Hessayon
THE WORLD'S BEST-SELLING BOOK ON GARDEN CONSTRUCTION

The **GARDEN REVIVAL EXPERT**
Dr. D. G. Hessayon
How to restore or change anything from a single shrub to your entire garden

The **GREENHOUSE EXPERT**
Dr. D. G. Hessayon
THE WORLD'S BEST-SELLING BOOK ON GREENHOUSES

The **HOUSE PLANT EXPERT**
Dr. D. G. Hessayon
THE WORLD'S BEST-SELLING BOOK ON HOUSE PLANTS

The **HOUSE PLANT EXPERT** Dr. D. G. Hessayon
BOOK TWO
THE MUST-HAVE SEQUEL TO THE WORLD'S BEST-SELLING HOUSE PLANT BOOK

The **LAWN EXPERT**
Dr. D. G. Hessayon
THE WORLD'S BEST-SELLING BOOK ON LAWNS

The **ORCHID EXPERT**
Dr. D. G. Hessayon
NAME THAT ORCHID – AND GET IT TO FLOWER AGAIN AND AGAIN

The **PEST & WEED EXPERT**
Dr. D. G. Hessayon

The **ROCK & WATER GARDEN EXPERT**
Dr. D. G. Hessayon
THE WORLD'S BEST-SELLING BOOK ON ROCK & WATER GARDENS

The **ROSE EXPERT**
Dr. D. G. Hessayon
THE WORLD'S BEST-SELLING BOOK ON ROSES

The **TREE & SHRUB EXPERT**
Dr. D. G. Hessayon
THE WORLD'S BEST-SELLING BOOK ON TREES & SHRUBS

The **VEGETABLE & HERB EXPERT**
Dr. D. G. Hessayon
THE WORLD'S BEST-SELLING BOOK ON VEGETABLES & HERBS

The **EXPERT VEGETABLE NOTEBOOK**
Dr. D. G. Hessayon
Begins by helping you choose and care for your plants...
Ends by providing a permanent record of your growing year

The Expert story

In 1958 a young botanist had the idea for a new type of gardening book. No long columns of type, no collection of coloured plates at the end and no technical terms which only the dedicated gardener would understand. The idea became reality and in the following spring *Be Your Own Gardening Expert* by Dr D G Hessayon appeared — a 36 page staple-bound "flattie" with coloured charts, annotated diagrams and an array of small blocks of down-to-earth information. Just a modest guide priced 1/6 (7$\frac{1}{2}$p), but it became the gardening best-seller of the year. *Be Your Own House Plant Expert* followed in 1960, a book which after a series of enlargements was destined to become the world's best-selling horticultural book.

There were more flatties to come — *Be Your Own Lawn Expert, Be Your Own Rose Expert* etc, and after 20 years the sales of these 32- and 64-page staple-bound books had reached 15 million. But now it was time for the *Be Your Owns* to grow up, and so in 1980 *The House Plant Expert* appeared — a 128 page paperback with its name on the spine. Now the books began to appear regularly each spring. Ten more Experts in the new enlarged style were published during the 1980s, and two of them appeared in the book list top 10 for the decade. It was during this period that they became firmly established as the gardening bibles, dominating the gardening book best-seller list on a regular annual basis.

The 1990s saw a stream of new titles — *The Flowering Shrub Expert, The Greenhouse Expert, The Bulb Expert, The Fruit Expert*, and so on. During this period the first two mega titles, the 256-page *Flower Expert* and *New House Plant Expert* were published. This decade also saw a rapid rise in the sale of Experts overseas — millions were sold in the U.S, and nearly a score of foreign language editions appeared. As the 50th birthday of the Experts approached Dr Hessayon produced yet another two titles — *The Pest & Weed Expert* and *The Orchid Expert*. On the 50th Anniversary of the writing of the first page the 50th million Expert was sold, and more new titles as well as updated editions are planned.

There are now 23 Experts in print, and there have been many changes over the past half century. But the basics used in the first slim volume remain. There have been awards along the way — a Lifetime Achievement "nibbie" from the National Book Awards, a Lifetime Achievement Award from the Garden Writers' Guild, an RHS VMM Medal, a Guinness World Record Certificate, an OBE and so on, but it is the Expert which is the celebrity and not the author. The most cherished honour an Expert receives is to hear a grandfather or grandmother say that it was receiving one of the slim *Be Your Owns* when he or she was a child which sparked a lifelong interest in gardening.

Shrubs for a shady site

Aucuba japonica
Camellia species
Fatsia japonica
Hypericum calycinum
Ligustrum species
Lonicera nitida
Mahonia aquifolium
Osmanthus heterophyllus
Prunus laurocerasus
Prunus lusitanica
Rubus species
Skimmia japonica
Symphoricarpos species
Viburnum davidii
Vinca species

Tying tips

- Many types of proprietary ties are available but soft string is as successful as any
- Tying properly involves attaching the stem to the support before the plant has started to flop. It is also necessary to attach the stem quite loosely
- When training climbers on to trellis, wires etc you should not tie the stems vertically — spreading them at first horizontally to form an espalier or at an angle to form a fan can dramatically increase the display
- Tying trees to stakes is more complex than dealing with flower and vegetable stems. You should wrap a short band of sacking around the trunk before tying with tarred string. Alternatively you can use an expanding tie. Tighten after a few weeks
- When a tree has outgrown its stake it may still need support. This can be provided by fixing a collar to the middle of the trunk and then securing it with 3 strong wires which are secured to the ground

Anatomy of a bird-friendly garden

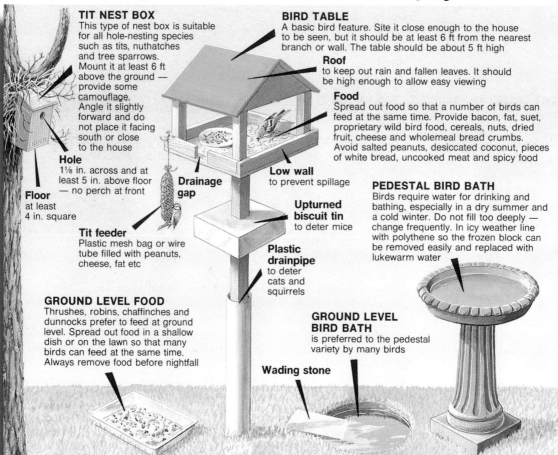

TIT NEST BOX
This type of nest box is suitable for all hole-nesting species such as tits, nuthatches and tree sparrows. Mount it at least 6 ft above the ground — provide some camouflage. Angle it slightly forward and do not place it facing south or close to the house

Hole
1⅛ in. across and at least 5 in. above floor — no perch at front

Floor
at least 4 in. square

Tit feeder
Plastic mesh bag or wire tube filled with peanuts, cheese, fat etc

Drainage gap

BIRD TABLE
A basic bird feature. Site it close enough to the house to be seen, but it should be at least 6 ft from the nearest branch or wall. The table should be about 5 ft high

Roof
to keep out rain and fallen leaves. It should be high enough to allow easy viewing

Food
Spread out food so that a number of birds can feed at the same time. Provide bacon, fat, suet, proprietary wild bird food, cereals, nuts, dried fruit, cheese and wholemeal bread crumbs. Avoid salted peanuts, desiccated coconut, pieces of white bread, uncooked meat and spicy food

Low wall
to prevent spillage

Upturned biscuit tin
to deter mice

Plastic drainpipe
to deter cats and squirrels

PEDESTAL BIRD BATH
Birds require water for drinking and bathing, especially in a dry summer and a cold winter. Do not fill too deeply — change frequently. In icy weather line with polythene so the frozen block can be removed easily and replaced with lukewarm water

GROUND LEVEL FOOD
Thrushes, robins, chaffinches and dunnocks prefer to feed at ground level. Spread out food in a shallow dish or on the lawn so that many birds can feed at the same time. Always remove food before nightfall

GROUND LEVEL BIRD BATH
is preferred to the pedestal variety by many birds

Wading stone

Caring for your moth orchid

PHALAENOPSIS

Typical Flower Form
Numerous flowers borne along arching spikes

All colours except blue

Flat-faced rounded shape

3-lobed lip

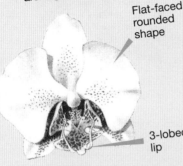

Pronunciation: fal-ee-**NOP**-sis

Common Name(s): Moth Orchid

Abbreviation: Phal.

Growth Type: Monopodial

Natural Habitat: On trees (rarely rocks) in tropical Asia and Australia

Ease of Cultivation: Easy

Flowering Season: No special season — can occur at any time. A collection can provide year-round flowers

Light: Reasonably bright light, but away from direct sunlight

Temperature: Warm conditions — low temperature will inhibit flowering

Watering: Year round. Compost should be kept moist, but never let it become waterlogged

Resting Period: Not needed, but a few weeks of cooler conditions at about 60°-65°F (16°-18°C) in autumn is useful

Phalaenopsis 'Cooks Pink'

Planting brassicas

① 4 in.

② Insert dibber
Insert plant
2 in.

③ Press towards plant

④ Tug test: Test one plant — leaf should tear before plant is uprooted

Rockery rejects

For nearly 100 years fanciful names have been given to poorly-designed rockeries. Despite changes in taste the two examples shown below have always been criticised by designers and yet are still found in gardens today.

The Currant Bun

The Dog's Grave

Marigold (Tagetes) types

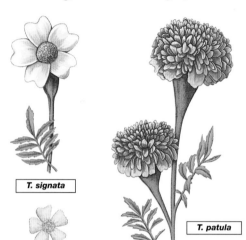

T. signata

T. signata 'Lemon Gem'
Tagetes

T. patula

T. patula 'Naughty Marietta'
French Marigold: Single group

T. patula 'Scarlet Sophia'
French Marigold: Double group

T. patula 'Tiger Eyes'
French Marigold: Crested group

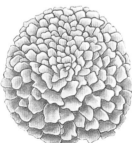

T. erecta 'Doubloon'
African Marigold

T. 'Nell Gwynn'
Afro-French Marigold: Single group

T. 'Sunrise'
Afro-French Marigold: Double group

Name that shrub

Medium shrub
•
Evergreen
•
Colour available

•
Flowering period

JANUARY
FEBRUARY
MARCH
APRIL
MAY
JUNE
JULY
AUGUST
SEPTEMBER
OCTOBER
NOVEMBER
DECEMBER

A shrub which is warmly recommended by all the experts. When not in flower it is a handsome rounded bush which is densely clothed with bright green and glossy foliage. Each evergreen leaf is made up of three leaflets. The main flush appears in May — flat heads of starry flowers with waxy petals and a strong Orange fragrance. A second smaller flush of flowers usually occurs in autumn, especially if the summer has been warm and dry. It is not a demanding plant — it will grow in acid or alkaline soil and does not mind some shade, but it is mildly sensitive to frost. In northern districts it is best to plant it against a wall.

Answer on page 128

Repairing concrete

The hollow must be at least ¹/₂ in. deep for filling. Cut round the edge with a club hammer and cold chisel. Remove some of the concrete within the hollow if the depression is less than the ¹/₂ in. minimum — remember to wear goggles. Clean the area, paint with dilute PVA adhesive and fill with a fairly dry concrete mix plus a little PVA adhesive, but wherever possible try to make up the same mixture used for making the path — getting a good colour match is a prime objective when filling concrete hollows. Smooth the surface with a float.

Fixing trellis

Step 2:
ATTACH THE TRELLIS TO THE BATTENS
Drill the trellis slats and then fasten with galvanised nails. With square mesh trellis fix the panel with horizontal slats facing outwards

Step 1:
PLACE SPACERS BETWEEN THE WALL AND TRELLIS
Do not attach trellis directly to the wall — a space here will allow plants to spread inside. In addition taking down the trellis will be much easier if pointing or decorating is required. One method of attachment is to fix a 1½ in. x 1½ in. batten to the wall with fibre-plugged brass screws — drill the battens before screwing. Place this first batten above at 3 ft intervals. Instead of battens you can use cotton reels or plastic tubes as spacers.

Gate hardware

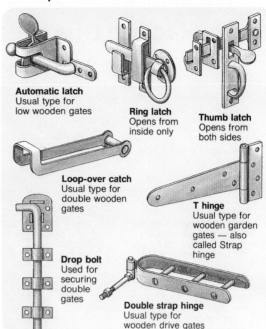

Automatic latch
Usual type for low wooden gates

Ring latch
Opens from inside only

Thumb latch
Opens from both sides

Loop-over catch
Usual type for double wooden gates

T hinge
Usual type for wooden garden gates — also called Strap hinge

Drop bolt
Used for securing double gates

Double strap hinge
Usual type for wooden drive gates

Rogues gallery

ROSE BLACK SPOT

The tell-tale signs are black spots with yellow edges. As the disease develops the yellow areas spread, premature leaf fall takes place and stems may die back. The fungus overwinters on stems and fallen leaves — infection takes place early in the season although the symptoms may not be clearly visible until July. The severity of the attack depends on the variety (shrub roses are usually less resistant than modern hybrids), the location (pure air encourages the disease) and the growing conditions (black spot thrives in warm, wet weather). It is difficult to control. Remove and burn fallen leaves and cut off black-spotted stems when pruning. Spraying is necessary with susceptible varieties. Apply myclobutanil when leaf buds are opening and repeat 7 days later. Spray again when first spots appear — repeat every 2 weeks. It is a mistake to wait until the spots appear before beginning to spray.

Planting a hanging basket

7 Water in the plants thoroughly but gently. Let the plants settle before placing outdoors — ideally the basket should be kept in the greenhouse or near a sunny window for about 2 weeks before hardening off and placing outdoors

6 Plant the centre of the basket with upright bedding plants — set trailing plants around the edge. Firm compost around the plants — there should be a 1 in. (2.5 cm) watering space between the compost surface and the top of the basket

5 Add more compost to near the top of the basket. Press down gently to compact the growing medium — this will reduce the speed of drying

3 Line the outside with a ½–1 in. (2 cm) layer of moist sphagnum moss. Place polythene sheeting over this layer and put a saucer at the bottom to hold it down

4 Half fill the basket with moist peat-based potting compost or Multicompost. Press down and then make 3–5 slits in the polythene at the compost surface level. Through each slit push a trailing plant seedling so that the soil ball rests on the compost and the top of the plant is beyond the sphagnum layer

2 A liner is required. This can be a pre-formed one (foam, cardboard or fibre) bought from your supplier. Many people prefer to use sphagnum moss which gives the basket a natural look, but rapid drying out and dripping can be problems. The sphagnum + polythene lining system is best — proceed to step 3

1 Filling a plastic basket is a simple matter — just place a few crocks above any drainage holes which may be present and then add a peat-based potting compost or Multicompost. Firm, and then go on to step 6. With a wire basket the situation is more complex. Begin by standing the container in a large pot or bucket for support. Go on to step 2

8 As with all containers the compost within the basket must not be allowed to dry out. Watering open baskets without a liner may be necessary every day or twice a day in summer — watering closed baskets with a drip tray will be required 2–3 times a week. Gently fill the watering space above the compost and allow to drain. Use steps to reach the basket for watering

9 Start to feed with a liquid fertilizer 6 weeks after planting. Repeat every 1–2 weeks as instructed on the pack. Use a fertilizer with a high potash content

10 Trim regularly to keep the plants in check and to remove dead blooms. If necessary peg down shoots with hair pins pushed through the lining and into the compost

Cabbage types

SPRING

SUMMER

WINTER

SAVOY

RED

CHINESE

House plant miscellany

POTTED HISTORY

The use of house plants to decorate rooms and hallways became a popular craze in the 19th century, but the house plant story is much older. It is known that plants were grown in pots by the Egyptians, Romans, Greeks and Chinese well before the birth of Christ, and it is assumed that many of these pots stood indoors. It could be that pots of herbs or garden flowers have stood on windowsills from time immemorial, but the story of growing exotics indoors really starts with the crusaders and then sailors bringing back specimens from the East in the 13th–15th century.

In the 17th and 18th century the aristocracy throughout Europe had their 'plant houses' with coal braziers or hot-air heaters for their oranges and other exotics, and in 1653 the first book to discuss gardening indoors (*The Garden of Eden*) appeared. Plants began to appear in the parlours of the wealthy, but the idea of using plants to furnish ordinary homes did not really take hold until the 1850s.

The first half of the 20th century was a quiet time for house plants. Between the wars there was little enthusiasm for filling the living room with all sorts of ironwork, pots and plants — few new plants or new ideas appeared. The end of World War II saw a renewed interest in indoor plants as harmful gas was replaced by electricity and central heating, and a flood of new varieties appeared.

Indoor plants in the 18th century home

POTTED PERFUME

A number of flowering house plants emit a distinct fragrance, ranging from the ones capable of filling a room with their heady aroma (Stephanotis, Lilium auratum etc) to the ones with a much more subtle fragrance (miniature Cyclamen, Exacum etc).

Two words of warning. Perfume is a highly personal thing, so the fragrance you may feel is wonderful may be unpleasant or even overpowering for your visitor. In addition it is usually unwise to have two or more scented plants growing close to each other. Despite these cautionary points the pleasant aroma of scented flowers is generally a welcome bonus and some suggestions are given below.

CITRUS	JASMINUM POLYANTHUM
CONVALLARIA	LILIUM (some)
CYTISUS CANARIENSIS	MANDEVILLA
DATURA	NARCISSUS (some)
EUCHARIS	NERIUM
FREESIA	OLEANDER
GARDENIA	ORCHID (some)
HOYA	PLUMARIA
HYACINTH	SPATHIPHYLLUM
IRIS RETICULATA	STEPHANOTIS

Erecting a fence post

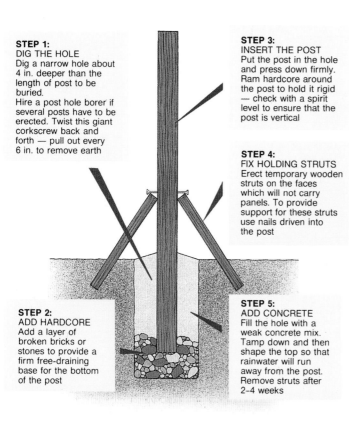

STEP 1:
DIG THE HOLE
Dig a narrow hole about 4 in. deeper than the length of post to be buried.
Hire a post hole borer if several posts have to be erected. Twist this giant corkscrew back and forth — pull out every 6 in. to remove earth

STEP 2:
ADD HARDCORE
Add a layer of broken bricks or stones to provide a firm free-draining base for the bottom of the post

STEP 3:
INSERT THE POST
Put the post in the hole and press down firmly. Ram hardcore around the post to hold it rigid — check with a spirit level to ensure that the post is vertical

STEP 4:
FIX HOLDING STRUTS
Erect temporary wooden struts on the faces which will not carry panels. To provide support for these struts use nails driven into the post

STEP 5:
ADD CONCRETE
Fill the hole with a weak concrete mix. Tamp down and then shape the top so that rainwater will run away from the post. Remove struts after 2-4 weeks

METAL POST SPIKES

If the ground is firm you can avoid the trouble of digging and concreting by using metal post spikes as an alternative fixing method

1. Place a block of wood in the rectangular cup and drive the spike into the ground by hammering the block. Stop occasionally to check with a spirit level

2. When only the rectangular cup is visible, remove the block and insert the post. Secure it by screwing or clamping, depending on the type of spike used

Shrubs for heavy soil

Aucuba japonica
Berberis species
Chaenomeles species
Choisya ternata
Cornus species
Corylus species
Cotoneaster species
Forsythia species
Hypericum species
Mahonia species
Philadelphus species
Potentilla species
Pyracantha species
Ribes sanguineum
Skimmia japonica
Spiraea species
Symphoricarpos species
Viburnum species
Vinca species
Weigela species

Orchid miscellany

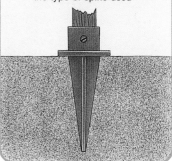

Untouched by human hand

Before independence berok monkeys were trained to collect orchids in Malaysia. These animals had been used for many years to gather coconuts in various countries, but orchid collect-ing was a specialised activity which called for a long period of training. The monkey clambered up the host tree after being told what to pick by its keeper, and it then brought down the epiphyte as instructed. The champion was Merah, who collected over 300 specimens in the 1930s.

Name that flower

Summer bedding plant
•
Hardy annual
•
Colours available

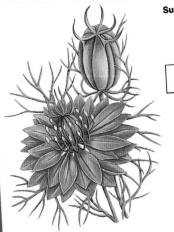

•

Flowering period

| JANUARY |
| FEBRUARY |
| MARCH |
| APRIL |
| MAY |
| JUNE |
| JULY |
| AUGUST |
| SEPTEMBER |
| OCTOBER |
| NOVEMBER |
| DECEMBER |

The blue varieties have been grown in gardens for hundreds of years, but these days you are more likely to find a multicoloured mixture listed in the catalogue. It is an easy plant to grow and is quite undemanding, but for top results you should incorporate organic matter in the soil before planting and dead blooms should be cut off to prolong the flowering season. Even with care this season will not be long — 6–8 weeks at best.

Answer on page 128

Disbudding

In general flower buds in the garden are allowed to develop and open naturally to provide the maximum display. For exhibitors, however, and others interested in the size of individual blooms, the flower-stems are disbudded. This calls for pinching out side buds as soon as they can be handled, leaving the central bud to develop into a large specimen to catch the eye of the judge or earn the envy of the neighbours.

Chrysanthemums, Dahlias and Carnations are frequently treated in this way for Show purposes. Many Hybrid Tea Roses produce more than one flower bud at the end of each shoot. With this flower it is nearly always desirable to seek maximum size, so disbudding of side shoots is recommended. Delay removing the side buds if you want to hold back flowering for the day of the Show. If the Rose variety produces very full blooms which spoil badly in wet weather, reverse the process and pinch out the terminal bud so that the side buds develop.

Apple & pear bud stages

BUD SWELLING		**BLOSSOM TIME** Early to mid May (Apples) Late April to early May (Pears)	
BUD BREAK			
BUD BURST		**PETAL FALL** When nearly all petals have fallen	
MOUSE EAR			
GREEN CLUSTER		**FRUITLET** Mid June	
PINK BUD (Apples) **WHITE BUD** (Pears)		**FRUITLET** Early July	

Pruning methods

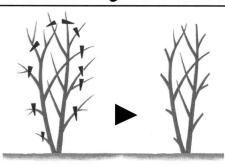

Heading back
The ends of the branches are removed
This may be the removal of just tips or practically all the stems (coppicing or pollarding). The immediate effect is to produce a shrub which is smaller than before. But the buds below the cut are then stimulated and will burst into growth so the long-term effect is to produce a tree or shrub which is bushier and leafier than one left unpruned

Shearing
All the growing points with only a small amount of stem attached are removed by cutting with shears or a hedge trimmer. This technique is used to maintain the shape of hedges and topiary

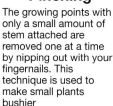

Pinching
The growing points with only a small amount of stem attached are removed one at a time by nipping out with your fingernails. This technique is used to make small plants bushier

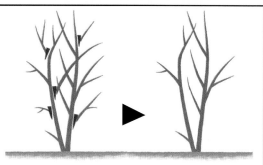

Thinning
Entire branches are cut right back to the main stem
This may be the removal of just one or two branches or the removal of all the branches from the main stem below the crown to produce a standard tree. The immediate effect is to direct extra energy to the remaining branches. Their growth will be accelerated, so the long-term effect is to produce a tree or shrub which is bigger and more open than one left unpruned

Lopping
The removal of a large branch from the trunk of a tree
Make a smooth sloping cut beyond the raised ridge (branch collar) at the base of the branch — leaving the collar on the tree will speed up healing. Begin by making a shallow cut on the underside, then saw downwards to sever the branch. Consider using a tree surgeon if the branch is heavy or out of reach

Lettuce types

COS (ROMAINE)

BUTTERHEAD

CRISPHEAD

LOOSE LEAF

Using your barbecue

The unique flavour of barbecued meat, fish and poultry is derived in 2 or 3 ways. With charcoal some of the taste comes from wood smoke — for maximum smoky flavour soak hickory or mesquite chips in water and sprinkle a thin layer on to the hot charcoal. With all barbecues much of the flavour is due to the smoke arising from hot fat dripping on to the charcoal or lava rock. Finally there is the taste of the barbecue sauce which is basted on to the food during the cooking process. Many barbecue enthusiasts have their own special (and secret) recipe for this sauce, but for most others the shop-bought bottled variety is quite satisfactory.

To light your charcoal fire use firelighter blocks with small pieces of charcoal on top, or soak lumps in lighting fluid for about $1/2$ hour before lighting. Do not begin cooking before the flames have died down and the charcoal pieces have a cover of grey ash.

Soaking meat in a marinade overnight will both tenderise and give more flavour to the food. The base of a marinade is usually beer, wine or lemon juice.

There are 4 basic long-handled utensils — tongs, fork, basting brush and turner. You will also need a poker for a charcoal barbecue. For the really keen there are all sorts of other items — broilers, skewers, thermometers and so on.

When cooking is finished leave charcoal to burn out and cool down — with gas models the lid should be closed and the gas turned on for about 5-10 minutes to burn off the grease. Clean the grill and tray as soon as they are cool and store indoors. Keep portable barbecues in a shed or garage to protect them from the rain.

Soak wooden skewers in water overnight before using for kebabs. This will reduce the risk of the wood scorching or igniting.

How to make an Ivy tree

Cut the side shoots from a specimen of Fatshedera lizei and stake the stem. When it has reached 3 ft high remove the top growth with a horizontal cut. Make crossed cuts on stem top as shown below.

4 Ivy cuttings inserted into cut stem and bound with raffia

1 inch-deep cuts

Watering the lawn

During a period of drought there is at first a loss of springiness in the turf and a general dullness over the surface. Later on the grass turns straw-coloured and unsightly. Before this stage you should have increased cutting height and the interval between mowings, and you will have to choose between two courses of action. First, you can decide to leave it to nature. Lawn grasses are very rarely killed by drought and recover quite quickly once the rains return. Watering is the alternative course of action, but it must be thorough. This calls for applying at least 20 litres per sq.m once a week until the dry spell ends. Do not use a hose pipe propped on the handle of a spade — water with a sprinkler so that a large area is covered. Do not try to take a middle course of action by sprinkling every few days to dampen the surface — this may do more harm than good.

Why trees & shrubs die

• Old age
Some trees like oaks and yews can live for hundreds of years, but there are a few shrubs such as broom which may die after a few years for no apparent reason.

• Poor site preparation
A shrub or tree growing in poorly-drained soil is likely to succumb to root-rotting diseases.

• Fatal diseases
Die-back, silver leaf, fireblight, clematis wilt, honey fungus, dutch elm, canker and butt rot can all kill susceptible plants.

• Wind rock
A serious problem on exposed sites. Staking of tall specimens until they are fully established is essential in these locations.

• Winter damage and Spring scorch
An abnormally severe winter can cause heavy losses, especially if the plants are evergreen and rather tender. Bright sunny weather after a cold spell can lead to the death of evergreens.

• Poor planting material
There are two serious conditions to watch for. Large girdling roots may wrap around the soil ball if the plant has been in the container for a prolonged period — this inhibits further root development. Another situation which can lead to early death is the drying out of the root system before planting.

• Poor planting
Failure to water in thoroughly, allowing the soil ball to break, and planting without firming the compost around the roots can all lead to early death.

• Water shortage
It is vital to make sure that trees and shrubs are watered in prolonged dry weather during the first season in the garden.

• Poor choice
Growing a sun lover in shade or an acid lover in chalky soil is a recipe for failure.

• Rabbits and Deer
These animals can cause havoc with young stock in rural areas — tree guards are the answer.

Anatomy of a path

Lawn edging
The path surface should be about 1 in. below the lawn so that the mower can run over the edge without damage. A clear grass-free strip or mowing edge should be maintained to make trimming easier

Rigid paving
Flagstones, paving slabs, paving blocks etc are bedded in mortar on top of the foundation. The advantages are strength and rigidity — essential in a driveway where a vehicle may be parked

Flexible paving
Bricks or paving blocks are pressed firmly into the sand-bed and extra sand is then brushed over the surface. The advantage is the ability to lift and replace small areas

Border edging
Many types of edging are available.
A firm edge is essential when gravel, bark chippings, bricks or blocks are used to prevent the movement of the paving material on to the adjacent soil. It is also desirable with all types of paths so that soil from beds and borders does not move on to the paving

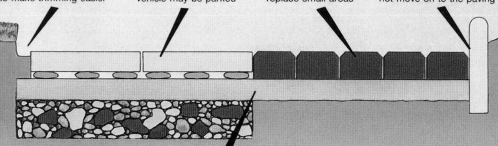

Foundation
The secret of long-lasting success is a firm foundation. The depth and construction of this base depend on the weight of traffic to be borne, soil type and the paving material chosen. The soil below the foundation must be thoroughly consolidated. A typical **rigid paving foundation** is 2–4 in. of hardcore below a 2 in. layer of compacted sand. For a driveway it may be necessary to have a concrete base. A typical **flexible paving foundation** is a 2 in. layer of compacted sand

Rogues gallery

CARROT FLY

The tell-tale sign is reddish foliage which wilts in sunny weather — at a later stage the leaves turn yellow. The 5 mm maggots are a serious pest of carrot, parsnip and celery — seedlings are killed, mature roots are riddled. Delay sowing maincrop carrots until June — lift as soon as practical. Sow thinly — destroy all thinnings.

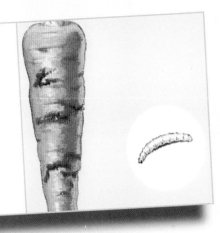

Easy-care border perennials

Fully hardy. Not prone to disease. No staking. No need to divide every few years

NAME	SITE	HEIGHT RANGE	FLOWERING TIME
ACHILLEA	Sun	60 cm - 1.2 m	June - Sept
AJUGA	Sun or light shade	15 cm	April - June
ALCHEMILLA	Sun or light shade	20 - 45 cm	June - July
ANEMONE	Sun or light shade	60 cm - 1.2 m	Aug - Oct
ARUNCUS	Light shade	90 cm - 1.8 m	June - July
ASTILBE	Light shade	60 - 90 cm	July - Aug
BERGENIA	Sun or light shade	30 cm	March - April
COREOPSIS	Sun	30 - 60 cm	July - Oct
DICENTRA	Light shade	30 - 60 cm	May - June
DORONICUM	Sun or light shade	30 - 90 cm	April - June
EUPHORBIA	Sun or light shade	10 cm - 1.5 m	April - May
GERANIUM	Sun or light shade	15 - 60 cm	July - Sept
HELLEBORUS	Partial shade	30 - 60 cm	Jan or March
HEMEROCALLIS	Sun or light shade	60 - 90 cm	June - Aug
HEUCHERA	Sun or light shade	40 - 60 cm	June - Aug
HOSTA	Partial shade	30 - 60 cm	June - Aug
IRIS	Sun	30 - 80 cm	Depends on species
NEPETA	Sun	20 - 60 cm	May - Sept
PRIMULA	Partial shade	30 - 60 cm	Depends on species
PULMONARIA	Partial shade	30 - 40 cm	April - May
RUDBECKIA	Sun or light shade	60 cm - 1.5 m	July - Oct
SEDUM	Sun	30 - 60 cm	Aug - Oct
SOLIDAGO	Sun	30 cm - 1.8 m	July - Sept
TRADESCANTIA	Sun or light shade	45 - 60 cm	June - Sept

Doronicum plantagineum

Geranium pratense

Hemerocallis 'Stafford'

Dianthus types

- Border perennial
- Bedding plant: half-hardy annual
- Bedding plant: hardy biennial
- Rockery perennial

PERENNIAL CARNATIONS

D. caryophyllus
Border Carnation

D. plumarius
Old-fashioned Pink

D. allwoodii
Modern Pink

ROCKERY PINKS

D. alpinus

ANNUAL & BIENNIAL CARNATIONS

D. barbatus
Sweet William

D. chinensis
Indian Pink

D. caryophyllus
Annual Carnation

Hardening off

Plants raised indoors or in a greenhouse have tender tissues — suddenly moving them outdoors in spring means a transition to colder conditions and drying winds for which they are not prepared. The result of this shock is either a severe check or death of the specimen, depending on the tenderness of the variety.

To avoid this problem there must be a gradual acclimatisation to the harsher conditions to be faced outdoors — a process known as hardening off. Begin by increasing the ventilation during the day in the greenhouse, after which the plants should be moved to a cold frame. Keep the lights closed at night for several days — then steadily increase the ventilation until the plants are continuously exposed to the outside air for a few days before planting out.

Watch the plants during hardening off. If the leaves turn blue or blotchy and growth stops you will have to slow down the process.

Storing furniture

Most folding furniture made of metal or wood is put away at night after use, together with cushions and covers. The reason is that damp-susceptible parts must be protected from dew, and wherever possible the furniture and furnishings should be allowed to dry before storage, especially if the material is ordinary fabric. With most folding chairs the proper way to fold them is obvious, but with director chairs it must be remembered that both the seat and fabric back should be lifted forward so that the cloth is not trapped by the wooden parts.

At the end of the summer most furniture is put away in the garage or shed — the only items which can be considered truly sun, frost and rainproof are non-folding items made of moulded resin, hardwood or cast aluminium. In addition genuine cast iron has good weather-resisting properties. Before items are put away in a dry place, some treatment and oiling may be necessary. Make sure all screws are tight — treat a loose rivet by placing the base on a solid surface and hitting the head of the rivet with a hammer.

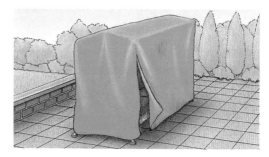

It is not always possible to move weather-susceptible items under cover in winter, and that means that chairs and hammocks with metal springs and rivets can rust badly. The answer is to buy waterproof woven polythene covers, as illustrated above.

Making a seat/planter

STEP 2:
ADD THE FINAL TOUCHES
When the final course of blocks has been laid, add the line of paving slabs to serve as seating and complete the planter with coping blocks — cut to fit. Leave to dry for a couple of days before using the seat — add cushions for comfort. Fill the planter with compost

STEP 1:
BUILDING THE STONE FRAMEWORK
Draw a plan to fit your patio. The seat should be about 1½ ft high and 1½ ft square. Paving slabs can be used as seating material. The planter should be 2½–3 ft high. The base must be firm and level. Use reconstituted stone blocks and thin layers of mortar, leaving weep-holes at the base of the planter

Why trees fail to fruit properly

• No pollination partner
A fine show of blossom every year which then fails to set fruit is generally caused by the absence of a pollination partner nearby. Plant a suitable variety — see The Fruit Expert for recommendations.

• Poor pruning or Careless picking
Over-vigorous pruning of a mature tree will result in abundant growth in the following season, and this will be at the expense of fruiting. Another mistake is cutting back lateral branches from a variety which bears its fruit on the shoot tips. Pulling unripe fruit off the spurs can cause damage and so limit next year's crop.

• Poor spring weather
The effect of a severe frost on open blossom can greatly reduce the crop — this is more likely to occur with pears rather than apples. Very dry air can result in poor pollination, and a wet, cold spring reduces the activity of pollinating insects.

• Overcropping
An apple tree can only support a limited number of large and well-shaped fruit. A heavy crop on the tree after the natural June drop should be thinned or the resulting fruit will be small and next year's crop will be light. Use scissors to remove small and damaged fruits to leave 2 apples per truss.

• Biennial bearing
Some varieties have a tendency to crop heavily one season and then very lightly 12 months later. If biennial cropping is a problem, rub away about half of the fruit buds from the spurs in spring before the expected heavy-cropping season.

• Impatience
You will not obtain high yields from an apple or pear tree until it is 5-7 years old.

• Pests and diseases
Apple troubles which can reduce yield include canker, brown rot and birds. Blossom wilt is a serious disease of plums.

• Poor location or Poor planting
Waterlogging and poor soil result in disappointing yields. There is little you can do with an established tree — the problem should have been tackled at the start. Other poor areas are exposed sites, hilly locations and sunless spots.

• Overvigorous growth
Lush leaf and stem growth with little or no blossom can be caused by feeding too much nitrogen or by pruning too severely. A high-potash fertilizer might help or you can try growing grass around but not up to the tree.

Flower arranging styles : 1

The MASS Style

Little or no open space is enclosed within the boundary of the arrangement — any space present is not a basic requirement of the style. The Mass style originated in Europe, beginning according to tradition with the Renaissance and first glorified in the paintings of the Dutch Masters in the 17th century. The style came into full flower with the table and room arrangements of the late Victorian era — silver trumpets packed with flowers and foliage, roughly oval in outline and often a kaleidoscope of colour. The 20th century has been a period of modification — the triangle has become the most popular shape and arrangements have become much looser and less formal.

The Mass style has several basic features. Generally the arrangement is an all-round one, and line material is used to create a skeleton of an upright axis and several horizontal laterals. This framework is then more or less completely covered with flowers and/or other plant material. There is usually no attempt to make any particular part a distinct focal point and transition is considered important. Transition means that changes within the arrangement are gradual rather than abrupt — colours, shapes etc of neighbouring blooms tend to blend together rather than stand out in sharp contrast. In the 1980s the Natural approach became popular — plant material is massed together "like flowers in the garden, with enough space for the butterflies."

The right spot for roses

PLENTY OF SUN is required to produce top quality roses, but light shade during the afternoon is beneficial.
ROSES CANNOT STAND DEEP AND CONTINUOUS SHADE

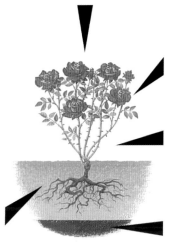

SUITABLE SOIL is necessary, and fortunately this can be achieved in nearly all gardens. Ideally it should be a medium loam, slightly acid and reasonably rich in plant foods and humus. A high clay content is not desirable (add organic matter) and a high lime content is harmful. Soil in which roses have grown for more than 5 years is liable to be 'rose sick' which means that new roses will not thrive after planting. Where possible choose a spot in which roses have not grown before, but this is not always possible. To reduce the chance of rose sickness when planting in a rose bed add a bark-based compost to the soil before planting and apply a hoof and horn fertilizer.
ROSES CANNOT THRIVE IF THE SOIL IS POOR

PLENTY OF AIR is required to produce healthy plants. Bush and standard roses do not like being shut in by walls and overhanging plants.
ROSES CANNOT STAND BEING PLANTED UNDER TREES

SHELTER FROM COLD WINDS is helpful. A nearby hedge or fence is useful, but it should not be close enough to shade the bush. Avoid planting in the lowest part of the garden if it is a 'frost pocket'.
ROSES DO NOT THRIVE IN EXPOSED SITES

REASONABLY FREE DRAINAGE is essential, so break up the subsoil if necessary.
ROSES CANNOT STAND BEING WATERLOGGED

Anatomy of a rockery

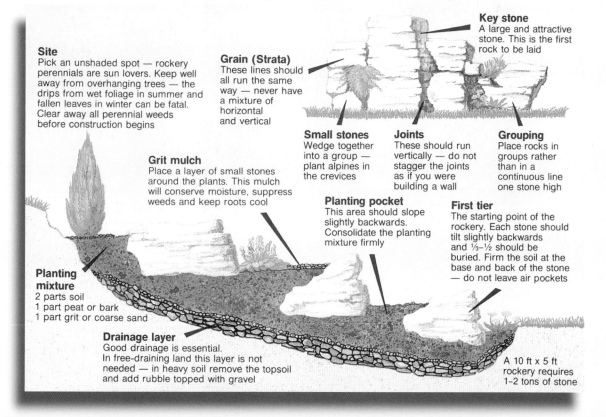

Site
Pick an unshaded spot — rockery perennials are sun lovers. Keep well away from overhanging trees — the drips from wet foliage in summer and fallen leaves in winter can be fatal. Clear away all perennial weeds before construction begins

Grain (Strata)
These lines should all run the same way — never have a mixture of horizontal and vertical

Key stone
A large and attractive stone. This is the first rock to be laid

Small stones
Wedge together into a group — plant alpines in the crevices

Joints
These should run vertically — do not stagger the joints as if you were building a wall

Grouping
Place rocks in groups rather than in a continuous line one stone high

Grit mulch
Place a layer of small stones around the plants. This mulch will conserve moisture, suppress weeds and keep roots cool

Planting pocket
This area should slope slightly backwards. Consolidate the planting mixture firmly

First tier
The starting point of the rockery. Each stone should tilt slightly backwards and $\frac{1}{3}$–$\frac{1}{2}$ should be buried. Firm the soil at the base and back of the stone — do not leave air pockets

Planting mixture
2 parts soil
1 part peat or bark
1 part grit or coarse sand

Drainage layer
Good drainage is essential. In free-draining land this layer is not needed — in heavy soil remove the topsoil and add rubble topped with gravel

A 10 ft x 5 ft rockery requires 1-2 tons of stone

Frost

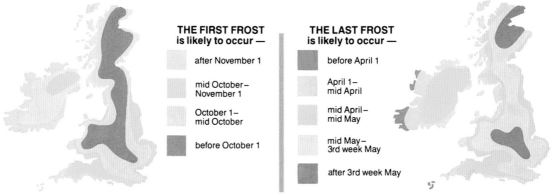

THE FIRST FROST is likely to occur —

after November 1

mid October–November 1

October 1–mid October

before October 1

THE LAST FROST is likely to occur —

before April 1

April 1–mid April

mid April–mid May

mid May–3rd week May

after 3rd week May

◀ **Hardy Plants** will survive in the garden during the period between the first frosts in autumn and the last frosts in spring. **Half-hardy Plants** are killed during this period if left unprotected outdoors. ▶

A frost occurs when the temperature falls below 32°F (0°C). It is damaging to plants in two ways — water is rendered unavailable to plant roots and the cells of sensitive plants are ruptured. These dangers are linked with the severity and duration of the frost as well as the constitution of the plant — in Britain we leave our Roses unprotected over winter whereas in some parts of Scandinavia and N. America straw or sacking protection is essential.

Late spring frosts which occur after growth has started are the most damaging of all. The danger signs are clear skies in the evening, a northerly wind which decreases at dusk and a settled dry period during the previous few days. The risk to a plant is reduced if there are overhanging branches above, other plants around, heavy soil below and the coast nearby.

In frost-prone areas avoid planting fruit trees and delicate shrubs. Provide some form of winter protection for choice specimens.

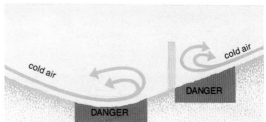

A frost pocket is an area which is abnormally prone to early autumn and late spring frosts. It occurs where a solid barrier is present on a sloping site — replace with an open barrier which allows air drainage. A frost pocket is also formed in the hollow at the bottom of a sloping site.

Perennial vegetables

NAME	NOTES
ASPARAGUS	Asparagus is not usually listed as an easy crop — free-draining soil, ample space and thorough bed preparation are necessary. Once established, however, it is easy to care for. Plant 1-year-old crowns 8 in. (20 cm) deep and 15 in. (37.5 cm) apart
EGYPTIAN ONION	The Egyptian or tree onion is an unusual plant which produces small onions instead of flowers on 3 ft (90 cm) stalks. Plant bulbils 9 in. (22.5 cm) apart in well-drained soil in late summer — picking time is June–January
RHUBARB	Usually regarded as a 'fruit' but is really a vegetable. Plant sets (pieces of crown) in February–March — bud should be just below surface and plants set at 3 ft (90 cm) intervals. Pick in April–July
SEAKALE	Reputed to be fussy, but seakale will grow in any ordinary soil. Plant thongs (root cuttings) in March — set them 18 in. (45 cm) apart and 2 in. (5 cm) deep. In November cover each plant with a pot or bucket. Cut in April, cook like asparagus
WELSH ONION	The Welsh or Japanese bunching onion is an excellent evergreen substitute for spring onions. Clumps of 2 ft (60 cm) high hollow leaves are produced — cut as required. Sow seed thinly in March — thin to 9 in. (22.5 cm) spacings

Leaf edges

ENTIRE

CRENATE

SERRATE

Soil profile

TOPSOIL is the fertile and living part of the soil. It is fertile because it contains nearly all of the humus, and it is living because it supports countless bacteria, which change various materials into plant foods. This layer varies from 2 in. in chalky soils to several feet in old, well-tended gardens. **When digging, this layer should be turned over, not buried under the subsoil.**

SUBSOIL lies under the topsoil, and is relatively dead and starved. It can be recognised by its lighter colour, due to lack of humus. **When digging, it should not be brought to the surface.**

A **SOIL PAN** is a horizontal layer, on or under the soil surface, which prevents the free movement of air and water to the region below. A surface pan is formed by the action of heavy rain on certain soil types — remove by hoeing or forking. Cultivating to the same depth year after year can cause sub-surface pans — another cause is the leaching down of iron, aluminium and manganese salts to a level where they form a chemical pan. Break through sub-surface pans by double digging.

Planting trees

Bare-rooted Trees

Short stakes are preferred these days to the traditional long ones. Place on the side from which the prevailing wind blows.

2 Plant firmly. The stem should be about 8-10 cm away from the stake.

3 Use plastic or rubber ties. Fix ties, one near the top of the stake and a bottom one close to ground level. Leave loose at first and then tighten after a few weeks when the tree has settled. Adjust ties as stem thickens.

1 Drive stake in firmly — 50-60 cm should be below ground level.

Container-grown Trees

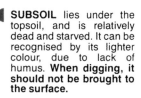

1 Plant firmly.

2 Drive the stake into the soil as shown, pointing into the prevailing wind.

3 Fix tie — adjust as the stem thickens.

Tufa

A truly surprising material. Tufa is a form of magnesium limestone which is porous and can hold more than its own weight of water — in addition plant roots will grow in it. A piece can be planted up with alpines and stood on a patio or balcony — the rock is soft and can be worked quite easily with a drill or chisel. Make a series of downward sloping holes 1 in. (2.5 cm) wide and 4 in. (10 cm) deep. Insert small rockery plants and plug in with a gritty compost. Keep the rock moist in dry weather.

Buying pot plants

Name that shrub

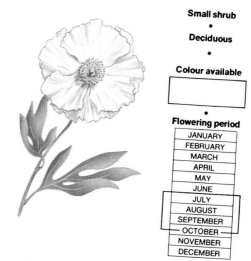

Small shrub
•
Deciduous
•
Colour available

Flowering period

JANUARY
FEBRUARY
MARCH
APRIL
MAY
JUNE
JULY
AUGUST
SEPTEMBER
OCTOBER
NOVEMBER
DECEMBER

From midsummer until autumn there are white fragrant Poppies which are 4–6 in. across, and the deeply cut leaves are an attractive shade of bluish-grey. The problem is that it is slow to establish, but once established it spreads quickly and can be invasive. Another problem is that some of the stems may be killed by frost, but new growth is rapidly produced.

Answer on page 128

Indoor plants are raised in glasshouses in which the air is warm and humid. The world outside is far less accommodating, so always buy from a reputable supplier who will have made sure that the plants have been properly hardened off. In this way the shock of moving into a new home will be reduced to a minimum.

House plants can, of course, be bought at any time of the year, but it is preferable to purchase delicate varieties between late spring and mid autumn. But some plants can only be bought in winter, and you should be extra careful at this time of the year. Plants stood outside the shop or on a market stall will have been damaged by the cold unless they are hardy varieties — avoid buying delicate plants which are stood in the open as 'bargain' offers.

Now you are ready to buy. If you are shopping for flower seeds, choose F_1 hybrids if available. If you are picking bulbs, make sure that they are firm, rot-free and without holes or shoots. When buying house plants, ensure that the specimen is not too big for the space you have in mind and then look for the danger signs. None present? Then you have a good buy.

Danger signs

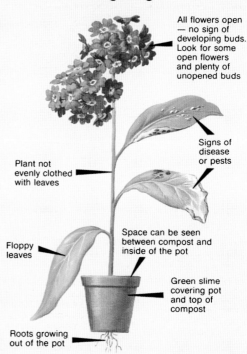

All flowers open — no sign of developing buds. Look for some open flowers and plenty of unopened buds

Signs of disease or pests

Plant not evenly clothed with leaves

Space can be seen between compost and inside of the pot

Floppy leaves

Green slime covering pot and top of compost

Roots growing out of the pot

Soil : the basic ingredients

MINERAL PARTICLES

The non-living skeleton of the soil which is derived from the decomposition of rocks by weathering. The fertility and size of these particles are governed by the type of parent rock.

Particle name is based on size. All **sands** have a gritty feel — **coarse sand** (0.6–2.0 mm in diameter) is distinctly gritty, **medium sand** (0.2–0.6 mm) feels like table salt and **fine sand** (0.02–0.2 mm) has a grittiness which is not easy to feel.

Silt (0.002–0.02 mm) has a silky or soapy feel. **Clay** (less than 0.002 mm) feels distinctly sticky.

AIR

Air is essential for the support of plant life and desirable soil life — it is also required for the steady breakdown of organic matter which releases nutrients. Movement of air is necessary to avoid the build-up of toxic gases — this air movement takes place through the soil pores.

HUMUS

Plant and animal remains are gradually decomposed in the soil. The agents of decay are the bacteria and other microscopic organisms. They break down dead roots and underground insects as well as fallen leaves carried below the soil surface by worms. Partially decomposed organic matter with the horde of living and dead bacteria is known as **humus** to the gardener. For the scientist it has a much narrower meaning. True humus is the dark, jelly-like substance which binds mineral particles into crumbs.

LIVING ORGANISMS

Millions of living organisms can be found in every ounce of soil. Most are microscopic — bacteria, fungi, eelworms etc. Others are small but visible — insects, seeds and so on. Worms and beetles are easily seen — the largest and least welcome living thing you are likely to find is the mole.

DEAD ORGANIC MATTER

The soil is the graveyard for roots, fallen leaves, insects etc as well as the organic materials (humus makers) we add to enrich it. Dead organic matter is *not* humus until it has decomposed. It does, however, serve as the base material for high bacterial activity and humus production. With this decomposition both major nutrients and trace elements are released into the soil. Some types of dead material may take many years to decompose.

STONES & GRAVEL

These are particles larger than 2 mm in diameter. 'Stones' usually refers to sizeable pieces of rock whereas 'gravel' usually describes the smaller weathered fragments — but there is no precise distinction.

WATER-BASED SOLUTION

This is often shortened to **soil water** but it is in fact a solution containing many dissolved inorganic and organic materials. Some (e.g nitrates, phosphates and potassium salts) are plant nutrients.

CRUMB

Crumbs range from lentil- to pea-sized. The spaces between them are known as **pores**.

Primula types

Bedding plant:
hardy annual
•
Border perennial
•
Bog plant
•
Rockery perennial

P. variabilis
Polyanthus

P. auricula
Auricula

P. japonica
Candelabra
Primrose

P. denticulata
Drumstick
Primrose

P. florindae
Giant Yellow
Cowslip

P. marginata
Rockery Primrose

Container problems

Make sure that the new container you have bought is satisfactory. Wooden ones should be watertight, terracotta ones should be resistant to frost if they are to be left outside all year round and all should have adequate drainage holes.

Containers do deteriorate with age and so regular maintenance is necessary. Cracked clay and terracotta pots are generally discarded, but with an expensive one you can remove a cracked section and glue it back with Superglue. Rust on metal containers should be dealt with promptly — treat with a tannin-based rust digester and then paint the surface. Softwood is always a problem — paint with a plant-safe preservative at regular intervals and replace any rotten sections which you find. Repairing chipped concrete or reconstituted stone is not easy — a mortar/PVA adhesive mix will be sound enough, but matching the colour is a problem. Finally, plastic and fibreglass. Plastic which has become brittle because of sunlight should be discarded, but kits are available for repairing damaged fibreglass.

Lawn stripes

A striped effect is sometimes regarded as a sign of a healthy and cared-for lawn, but it is nothing of the sort. It merely results from cutting the grass in parallel strips with a mower which is fitted with a roller. The alternate stripes are mown in opposite directions, and stripes are useful for masking small imperfections and colour variations. This is a technique for good drivers — it is unsightly if it is not done neatly and accurately.

Planting shrubs

TIMING

CONTAINER-GROWN PLANTS

JULY	AUG	SEPT	OCT	NOV	DEC	JAN	FEB	MARCH	APRIL	MAY	JUNE

BALLED EVERGREENS   **BARE-ROOTED PLANTS & PRE-PACKAGED PLANTS**   **BALLED EVERGREENS**

Container-grown plants can be planted at any time of the year, but it is advisable to avoid the depths of winter and midsummer if you can. The time for planting bare-rooted and pre-packaged plants is much more restricted. For most gardens the best time is between October and late November, but if the weather is abnormally wet or if the soil is heavy clay then it is better to wait until March. With balled evergreens the best time is early autumn (early September–mid October) — plant in April if you miss the autumn planting date. Soil conditions are as important as the calendar. The ground should be neither frozen nor waterlogged. Squeeze a handful of soil — it should be wet enough to form a ball and yet dry enough to shatter when dropped on to a hard surface.

SPACING

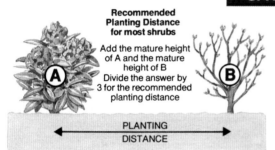

Recommended Planting Distance for most shrubs

Add the mature height of A and the mature height of B Divide the answer by 3 for the recommended planting distance

PLANTING DISTANCE

Planting too closely is a common problem. It is easy to see why people do this — the plants from the garden centre are usually small, and it is hard to imagine at this stage what they will look like when they are mature. When you plant at the recommended distances the border will look bare and unattractive. You can plant a little closer, but that is not really the answer. One solution is to plant a number of 'fill-in' shrubs between the choice shrubs you have planted. These 'fill-in' shrubs should be inexpensive old favourites (Forsythia, Spiraea, Ribes etc) and are progressively removed as the choice shrubs develop. A second alternative is to fill the space between the planted shrubs with bulbs, bedding plants or herbaceous perennials.

Rose colours

SINGLE COLOUR
Petals similarly coloured throughout, although some changes may occur as blooms get older.
Example: Iceberg

BI-COLOUR
Colour of the outside of each petal distinctly different from the inside hue.
Example: Piccadilly

MULTI-COLOUR
Colour of the petals changes distinctly with age. Flower trusses have several colours at the same time.
Example: Masquerade

BLEND
Two or more distinct colours merge on the inside of each petal.
Example: Peace

STRIPED
Two or more different colours on each petal, one of which is in the form of distinct bands.
Example: Rosa Mundi

HAND PAINTED
Silvery petals with red blotched and feathered over the surface, leaving a white eye at the base.
Example: Regensberg

Shrubs for wildlife

Bees   Birds   Butterflies

Aucuba

Berberis

Buddleia

Callicarpa

Ceanothus

Chaenomeles

Cistus

Clerodendrum

Cotinus

Cotoneaster

Cytisus

Daphne

Escallonia

Euonymus europaeus

Fuchsia

Hebe

Hippophae

Hypericum

Ilex

Lavandula

Ligustrum

Mahonia

Olearia

Pernettya

Perovskia

Potentilla

Pyracantha

Ribes odoratum

Sambucus

Skimmia

Spiraea

Symphoricarpos

Syringa

Ulex

Viburnum

Weigela

Earthing up

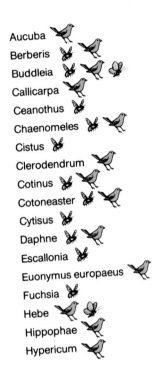

There are several reasons for earthing up — the drawing of soil towards and around the stems. Potatoes are earthed up to avoid the tubers being exposed to light. When the haulm is about 9 in. high a draw hoe is used to pile loose soil against the stems to form a flat-topped ridge. The greens (Broccoli, Kale, Brussels Sprouts etc) are earthed up for a different reason — soil is drawn up around the stems of well-developed plants to improve anchorage against high winds.

The stems of Celery and Leek are blanched by earthing up. This begins with Celery when it is about 1 ft high — with Leeks this is done in stages, the height being increased a little at a time by drawing dry soil around the stems.

Earthing up is important on the vegetable plot but it has a place in the herbaceous border. Shoots may appear prematurely during a mild spell in early spring — it is advisable to draw loose soil over them with a hoe so as to prevent damage by severe frosts which may come later.

Gloves & knives

The purpose of wearing **gloves** is not merely to keep your hands clean — a barrier cream applied before going out is the way to avoid soiling your skin. Leather gloves are used to protect the hands from prickles, sharp objects and caustic materials such as lime. But they are heavy, somewhat inflexible and uncomfortable in hot weather. Cotton gloves are much more comfortable, but are no protection against Rose thorns. A good compromise is to buy a pair of fabric gloves with leather palms or a pair of the popular fabric gloves impregnated with green plastic to give a protective suede-like finish.

It is a joy to watch a skilled gardener using a knife, but in the hands of the inexperienced it can be a dangerous weapon. If you have not been trained in its use carry a folding pocket knife for cutting twine etc, but use secateurs for cutting stems. Several types are available — a **pruning knife** has a curved blade and a **grafting knife** has a 3 in. straight one. A **budding knife** is smaller — the 2 in. long blade has a flat tip rather than a pointed one and the flattened handle is used for lifting the bark when budding.

Hiring people

Getting someone to help in the garden may sound like the answer to your prayers, but without forethought it can go wrong. Set out below are the things to look out for.

HIRING A GARDENER FOR GENERAL HELP

- Find out the hourly rate for your area by asking other people, and see if friends can recommend someone they have used
- If you have to find your own gardener then look through local papers or place your own advertisement in the press. Do not give work to people who knock at the door
- Agree the rate in writing and list the work that you will expect to be done
- There can be a tax problem. If you employ your helper for only a few hours a week there should be no problem, but a part-time gardener working just for you may be classed as an employee which will involve you in paying both PAYE and National Insurance. If in doubt, check with the Tax Office
- If you are disabled the local Council may provide garden help free of charge. Check with the Council Office

HIRING A CONTRACTOR FOR A SPECIFIC TASK

- If possible go to a company which has been highly recommended by someone with high standards
- If you have to find your own contractor look through Yellow Pages — get a quote from several if you can
- Agree the job in writing and be as specific as you can. Make sure the landscape contractor is insured and don't keep adding little bits to the job as the final price may go up alarmingly.

Fruit trees : planting material

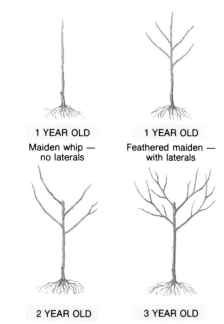

1 YEAR OLD	1 YEAR OLD
Maiden whip — no laterals	Feathered maiden — with laterals

2 YEAR OLD	3 YEAR OLD

1 year old 'maiden'	Untrained. You will have to prune for about 3 years to produce a satisfactory framework of branches
2 year old	Partly trained. You will have to continue training to produce a satisfactory framework
3–4 year old	Trained. Purpose of pruning will be to maintain balance between growth and fruitfulness
Over 4 year old	Generally too old for planting. Establishment may be very slow

Looking after tools

- Clean off all mud, grass etc after use — dry with a rag. Never allow grass mowings to dry on the blades of a mower — removing dried grass and earth with a knife is a laborious task.
- Wipe tools with an oily rag before storing them away — hoes, spades, forks, rakes and trowels can be pushed into a tub of oiled sand if no other method of storage is available.
- Keep hand tools off the floor of the garage or toolshed. Hang them on the wall if possible — keep sharp tools out of harm's way. Turn the lawnmower so that the blades are away from the line of traffic.
- Sharpen tools regularly. During winter look for rust on large and expensive equipment. Paint affected areas with an anti-rust paint to prevent further corrosion.

Rogues gallery

SPLITTING

Splitting is a common disorder of many vegetables. With some there is a simple cracking of the surface — commonly-seen examples are roots or tubers such as beetroots, carrots, swedes, turnips and potatoes. Other vegetables which may split are celery stalks, tomato fruits and cabbage hearts. The exposed areas are sometimes attacked by harmful fungi or bacteria. In a few cases splitting is not obvious from the outside — **saddleback** of onions (splitting at the base) is seen when the outer layers are peeled away and **hollow heart** of potatoes is only apparent when the tuber is cut in two. Although splitting affects a variety of plants in a number of ways the cause is nearly always the same — heavy rain or watering after a prolonged period of drought. Applying a mulch will help. Never keep the plants short of water during dry spells. Use split potatoes, carrots etc as soon as possible as they will not keep in store.

Carrot

Onion

When to prune roses

Prune at or before the recommended pruning date for your part of the country

- EARLY APRIL
- LATE MARCH
- MID MARCH

BUSHES, STANDARDS & CLIMBERS

Early spring pruning is recommended for autumn- and winter-planted roses and for established plants. If the bushes or standards are to be planted in the spring, prune just before planting.

The best time to prune is when growth is just beginning. The uppermost buds will have begun to swell but no leaves will have appeared.

One of the dangers of leaving pruning until spring is the possibility of wind-rock in the winter gales. Avoid this by cutting back long shoots in November.

RAMBLERS

Prune in late summer or autumn once flowering has finished.

Pruning too early may result in buds breaking prematurely in a mild spell, followed by frost injury if freezing weather returns.

Despite this possibility, some rose experts prune regularly during above-freezing weather in January or February and claim they obtain earlier flowering than with the more usual March pruning.

Pruning too late results in the plant being weakened. This is because the sap is flowing freely upwards once the buds are actively growing, and pruning at this stage is bound to cause considerable loss of sap.

Common garden weeds

AEGOPODIUM PODAGRARIA
(Ground elder)

The underground rhizomes spread among perennials and around shrubs. Divide affected perennials and remove runners from clumps — carefully dig out around shrubs or use glyphosate. An anti-weed mulch is the best idea.

AGROPYRON REPENS
(Couch grass)

This perennial grass is a common weed in beds, borders and paths. Clumps are easy to fork out, but remaining bits soon regrow. Susceptible to glyphosate when actively growing. Use an anti-weed mulch if a large area is affected.

CALYSTEGIA SEPIUM
(Hedge bindweed)

Pretty flowers, but the twining stems can swamp shrubs and perennials. The deep roots cannot be dug out and cutting back is quickly followed by regrowth. The best plan is to use the glyphosate glove technique — see page 120.

POA ANNUA
(Annual meadow grass)

An annual weed which grows everywhere and can become a menace if neglected. It looks delicate, but it can form a turf which is very difficult to dig out effectively. Spray or spot-treat with glyphosate or put down an anti-weed mulch.

TARAXACUM OFFICINALE
(Dandelion)

Too well-known to require description, a large patch of mature specimens is not easy to eradicate by digging out — regrowth occurs from root remnants. Spot-treating with glyphosate is effective — so is an anti-weed mulch.

URTICA DIOICA
(Stinging nettle)

An indicator of fertile soil. It spreads by means of underground and surface creeping stems — these must be removed when digging out isolated clumps. Treat large areas with glyphosate or put down an anti-weed mulch.

Border Iris types

RHIZOME GROUP

BEARDED IRISES

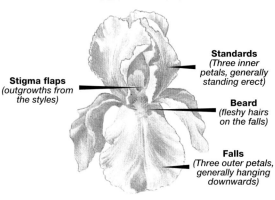

Standards
(Three inner petals, generally standing erect)

Stigma flaps
(outgrowths from the styles)

Beard
(fleshy hairs on the falls)

Falls
(Three outer petals, generally hanging downwards)

BEARDLESS IRISES

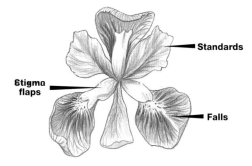

Standards

Stigma flaps

Falls

CRESTED IRISES

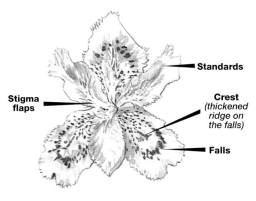

Standards

Stigma flaps

Crest
(thickened ridge on the falls)

Falls

Forking

A garden fork is not really a digging tool, although it can sometimes be easier to dig a heavy soil with a fork rather than a spade. Forking is really a method of cultivation — lumps are broken down by hitting them with the tines and the surface roughly levelled by dragging the tines across the surface. Forking is also used around growing plants to break up the surface crust.

Thinning

Thinning is carried out at several stages in the life cycle of some plants — from the time when they are seedlings to the fruiting period of large trees. Despite the often-repeated recommendation to sow thinly you will usually find that the seedlings emerging in the vegetable plot or in seed boxes are too close together. Thinning is necessary, and this is a job to be tackled as soon as the plants are large enough to handle. Delay means spindly plants which never fully recover. The soil should be moist — water if necessary. Hold down the soil around the unwanted seedling with one hand and pull it up with the other. If the seedlings are too close together to allow this technique, nip off the top growth of the unwanted ones and leave the roots in the soil. After thinning, firm the soil around the remaining seedlings and water gently.

Thinning out of stems may be necessary in the herbaceous border, and it is often required with ornamental and fruit trees when branches become overcrowded. Following the pruning of Roses it is often found that 2 or more shoots develop from a single bud behind the cut. Rub out the weaker shoot.

Several kinds of fruit trees and bushes some-times set a heavier crop than is required. Crowded fruits do not develop properly, and so thinning is required to allow the remaining ones to develop fully. Recommended distances between fruits are Peaches 9 in., Apples 6 in., Plums 3 in., Gooseberries 1 in. Grapes are thinned by removing some of the fruit with vine scissors from each bunch.

Container planting

Plan the design first if several plants are to be put into the container. Water the pots thoroughly and allow to drain before you begin. Make sure that the growing medium in the container is moist. Plants raised under glass should have been properly hardened off.

① Start with the largest plant. Dig a hole in the compost. Make sure that the hole is large enough for the rootball by inserting the pot into it — remove more compost if the pot does not fit easily

② Remove the plant from the pot. With container-grown plants cut down the side and remove cover carefully. Put the rootball in the hole — the top of the rootball should be at or just below the surface

③ Firm in by replacing some of the compost removed by the trowel and then pressing down with your fingers. Continue planting — finish off with the edging plants. Smooth the compost

④ Planting is now finished — note that any staking which is required should have been done before the plants were set in the holes. With permanent planting cover the top with chippings or bark. Water in gently

Fragrant shrubs

Many shrubs bear sweet-smelling flowers — Honeysuckle, Mock, Orange, Daphne, Viburnum and Witch Hazel are all well known for their perfume. Fragrance is not restricted to the flowers — some shrubs have aromatic foliage.

✿ *Fragrant flowers*

🍃 *Aromatic leaves*

Abelia chinensis ✿
Abeliophyllum distichum ✿
Acacia dealbata ✿
Akebia species ✿
Azara species ✿
Berberis stenophylla ✿
Buddleia alternifolia ✿
Buddleia davidii ✿
Buddleia globosa ✿
Callistemon species 🍃
Calycanthus species ✿ 🍃
Caragana arborescens ✿
Crapenteria californica ✿
Caryopteris clandonensis 🍃
Celastrus species ✿
Chimonanthus praecox ✿
Choisya ternata ✿ 🍃
Clematis montana ✿
Clerodendrum trichotomum ✿
Clethra alnifolia ✿

Coronilla glauca ✿
Corylopsis species ✿
Crataegus species ✿
Cytisus battandieri ✿
Daphne species ✿
Elsholtzia species 🍃
Escallonia macrantha 🍃
Eucryphia lucida ✿
Hamamelis species ✿
Hoheria species ✿
Itea species ✿
Jasminum species ✿
Lavandula species ✿ 🍃
Lonicera fragrantissima ✿
Lonicera periclymenum ✿
Lupinus arboreus ✿
Magnolia grandiflora ✿
Magnolia stellata ✿
Mahonia species ✿
Myrica species 🍃
Myrtus communis ✿ 🍃
Osmanthus species ✿
Passiflora caerulea ✿

Perovskia atriplicifolia 🍃
Philadelphus species ✿
Phlomis fruticosa 🍃
Pittosporum tobira ✿
Poncirus species ✿
Prunus lusitanica ✿
Rhododendron — deciduous Azaleas ✿
Ribes odoratum ✿
Romneys hybrida ✿
Rosa species ✿
Rosmarinus officinalis 🍃
Rubus tridel 'Benenden' ✿
Santolina species 🍃
Sarcococca species ✿
Skimmia japonica 🍃
Staphylea species ✿
Styrax species ✿
Syringa species ✿
Trachelospermum species ✿
Viburnum bodnantense ✿
Viburnum farreri ✿
Wisteria species ✿
Zenobia species ✿

House plant miscellany

DARK CORNER DILEMMA

It is a temptation to try to brighten up a dark corner with house plants, but there are questions to ask before you start. Is there enough light? To support any plant it should be possible to read a newspaper in the darkest part in late morning or early afternoon and the plants should cast at least a vague shadow on a bright day.

The test above will reveal whether there is enough light, but you will have to be careful when deciding what to grow. The choice will be limited if the corner is truly shady. In the list below you will find no flowering plants but there are a number of easily-available and attractive foliage ones.

It will help if the surface of the corner is papered or painted in white or a pale colour — a mirrored surface is even more helpful. The list of suitable plants will unfortunately not be enlarged — if you want to have flowers and/or a wider range of foliage plants, it will be necessary to take a different approach. You can use bright-light types for a few weeks and then move them to a bright location to recuperate for a week or two. An alternative route is to buy pots of brightly-coloured flowering types and treat them as a temporary display in the same way as you would treat a vase of cut flowers.

AGLAONEMA

ASPIDISTRA

ASPLENIUM (Bird's nest fern)

FICUS PUMILA (Creeping fig)

HEDERA (Ivy)

PELLAEA (Button fern)

PHILODENDRON SCANDENS (Sweetheart plant)

SANSEVIERIA (Snake plant)

SCINDAPSUS (Pothos)

SYNGONIUM (Goosefoot)

HANDLE WITH CARE

Very few house plants pose any problems, but it is useful to know which ones can have undesirable effects if eaten or handled.

CACTI	Hooked spines
DATURA	All parts poisonous
DIEFFENBACHIA	Poisonous sap
NERIUM	All parts poisonous
POINSETTIA	Irritating sap
PRIMULA OBCONICA	Irritating leaves
SOLANUM CAPSICASTRUM	Poisonous berries
YUCCA ALOIFOLIA	Sword-like leaves

Orchid miscellany

Darwin was right

It was Charles Darwin who first clearly demonstrated that orchids were adapted to be visited by specific moths, bats, birds etc which serve to pollinate them. However, he was sent a beautiful, large white orchid (**Angraecum sesquipedale**) from Madagascar which set him a puzzle. It had a 1 ft (30 cm) long spur which contained nectar — but no known moth had a proboscis that long. He predicted that it must exist, but most of his fellow naturalists laughed at the idea. About 40 years later it was indeed discovered — and named Xanthopan morganii praedicta in honour of his prediction.

Covering a shady wall

The number of plants which will thrive on a north-facing wall or solid fence is limited — tried and tested ones are listed below. The area immediately next to the wall is often dry because it is in a rain shadow — always leave at least 30 cm between the plant and the stone, brick or wood.

Hydrangea petiolaris • Lonicera japonica
Hedera spp • Polygonum baldschuanicum
Clematis montana • Parthenocissus spp
Jasminum nudiflorum • Akebia quinata

Gladiolus types

Bulb

LARGE-FLOWERED HYBRIDS

G. 'Flower Song'

PRIMULINUS HYBRIDS

G. 'Columbine'

BUTTERFLY HYBRIDS

G. 'Melodie'

SPECIES GLADIOLI

G. colvillei 'The Bride'

MINIATURE HYBRIDS

G. 'Greenbird'

Broad bean types

LONGPOD varieties (L)

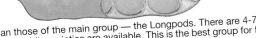

The long, narrow pods hang downwards, reaching 16in. or more in length. There are 8-10 kidney-shaped beans within each pod — both green and white varieties are available. This is the best group for hardiness, early cropping, exhibiting and top yields.

WINDSOR varieties (W)

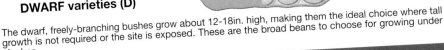

The pods are shorter and broader than those of the main group — the Longpods. There are 4-7 round beans within each pod — both green and white varieties are available. This is the best group for flavour. They are not suitable for autumn sowing and they take longer to mature than Longpods.

DWARF varieties (D)

The dwarf, freely-branching bushes grow about 12-18in. high, making them the ideal choice where tall growth is not required or the site is exposed. These are the broad beans to choose for growing under cloches.

Building a rock garden

1 **PLAN CAREFULLY** Careful planning is essential before you begin. Remember that the aim is to produce a rock garden which looks as natural as possible — avoid at all costs scattering stones at random over a flat bed. Choose one of the basics designs shown on page 89 — as a general rule a sloping rock garden is more attractive than a level one. The chosen site should be free from shade for most of the day — a background of trees and shrubs will improve the 'natural' feel, but trees must be far enough away to have no harmful effect on the plants. Visit a good rock garden or two to see how an outcrop or terraced rockery should look. Draw a rough sketch, but a detailed plan is impossible. Mark out an area with string which is slightly larger than the planned rock garden.

Some protection from northern winds

No overhanging trees

South or west

2 **PREPARE THE SITE** Choose a day when the soil is reasonably dry. Strip off turf if present and remove perennial weeds. This weed removal is absolutely vital as couch, bindweed etc can ruin a rock garden. Dig out the roots — if the site is badly infested you will have to use an appropriate weedkiller such as glyphosate and leave the site unplanted for the period recommended on the label. Good drainage is another vital need. With a sloping site in a non-clayey area no extra preparation will be required, but if the subsoil is heavy then a drainage layer will be necessary as shown on the right.

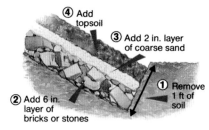

④ Add topsoil
③ Add 2 in. layer of coarse sand
① Remove 1 ft of soil
② Add 6 in. layer of bricks or stones

3 **MOVE THE STONES** You will be able to move small stones by simply carrying them, either alone or with assistance from a helper. Wear leather gloves and stout boots. Remember the golden rules — knees bent, back straight, hold the load evenly and then straighten knees with elbows close to your thighs, Never stoop over to grasp the rock and never jerk suddenly to raise it above ground. You will be able to tackle rocks weighing $1/2$-1cwt in this way, but in a large rockery you will need some stones which weigh appreciably more. One of the best aids for medium-sized rocks is a sack trolley — you will have to lay down a trackway of boards on soft ground. Do not use a single-wheeled garden wheelbarrow as the load can easily tip over. Some stones are too large for a sack trolley and these pose a problem. You can make a track of wooden planks and roll the rock along by turning it over with a crowbar, but it is often easier to use the method shown on the right.

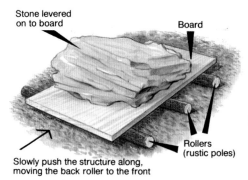

Stone levered on to board

Board

Rollers (rustic poles)

Slowly push the structure along, moving the back roller to the front

Greenhouse maintenance

There may be more to do than just cleaning the glass, framework, shelves, staging etc. Check all iron and steel fittings, hinges and screws for rust — if sound apply a thin film of oil. If corrosion is present, treat with a tannate-based rust destroyer before painting. Replace badly-rusted hinges.

Draughts are a special problem, as they are not only uncomfortable for you but they can be deadly for the plants. Check that vents and doors fit tightly — fit self-adhesive draught-proofing strips if they don't. Louvres are a common cause of draughts, so check them carefully.

Inspect the sides of the glasshouse if it is not glazed to the ground. Repoint brick walls as necessary and replace any boards which may be missing from a wooden base.

The wooden framework of the house should be inspected and the gutters will need cleaning and repairing if necessary. Check the wires used for supporting tall plants inside the house — these generally need replacing every few years. Replace broken or cracked panes and renew damaged or missing putty.

Name that flower

Garden/Indoor plant
•
True bulb
•
Colours available
•
Flowering period

| JANUARY |
| FEBRUARY |
| MARCH |
| APRIL |
| MAY |
| JUNE |
| JULY |
| AUGUST |
| SEPTEMBER |
| OCTOBER |
| NOVEMBER |
| DECEMBER |

This low-growing early spring bulb is a popular choice for naturalising in the rockery or grassland, but was not grown as a garden plant before the middle of the 19th century. The 6-petalled starry flowers are borne in loose and dainty sprays on upright flower stalks which rise above the strap-like leaves. The foliage withers and dies once flowering is over — the blooms last for 3-4 weeks and can be cut for indoor decoration. Indoors plant the bulbs in September for February flowers.

Answer on page 128

House plant design terms

BALANCE

There are two aspects to the concept of balance. The first one concerns the plant or plants in the receptacle. Here there must be physical balance, which means that the receptacle and its compost must be heavy enough to prevent a one-sided arrangement from toppling over. In addition there must also be visual balance, which means that a physically-stable feature must not *look* as if it could topple over. You can increase the 'weight' of the lighter side of a visually-unbalanced feature by introducing plants with large, dark leaves. The second aspect of balance concerns the visual impact of two nearby features, which may be quite different in style, against a wall. To see if they are balanced, imagine them on the pans of a giant pair of scales — if one side would clearly outweigh the other then the effect is not balanced.

Cauliflower types

SUMMER CAULIFLOWER

These cauliflowers mature during the summer months from seed sown in a cold frame in September, in a greenhouse or on the windowsill in January or outdoors in April. They are compact plants — you can choose an early variety, such as Snowball, which will produce heads in June or July, or you can grow a later-maturing type like All the Year Round which will be ready for cutting in August from an outdoor sowing.

AUTUMN CAULIFLOWER

These cauliflowers mature during the autumn months and are of two quite different types. There are the large and vigorous varieties such as Autumn Giant and Flora Blanca, and there are the more compact Australian varieties such as Canberra.

WINTER CAULIFLOWER

'Winter cauliflower' is a technically incorrect name. The standard types mature in spring not winter, and they are really heading broccoli. Although less delicately-flavoured than true cauliflowers the popular varieties of winter cauliflower are easier to grow.

Garden butterflies

Brimstone

Cabbage White

Comma

Common Blue

Holly Blue

Orange Tip

Painted Lady

Peacock

Red Admiral

Small Copper

Small Tortoiseshell

Wall Brown

Rogues gallery

HONEY FUNGUS

A common cause of the death of shrubs and trees. A white fan of fungal growth occurs below the bark near ground level. On roots black 'bootlaces' are found. Toadstools appear in autumn at the base. Burn diseased stems and roots and replace with non-woody types. The use of a phenolic soil drench is no longer permitted.

Watch that back!

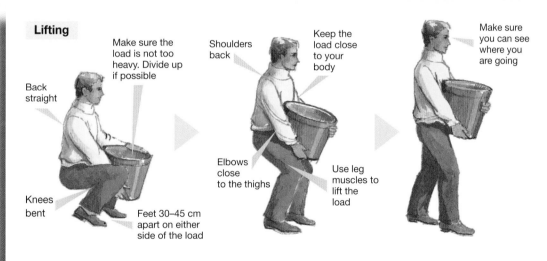

Lifting

Back straight

Make sure the load is not too heavy. Divide up if possible

Knees bent

Feet 30–45 cm apart on either side of the load

Shoulders back

Keep the load close to your body

Elbows close to the thighs

Use leg muscles to lift the load

Make sure you can see where you are going

Hoeing & Raking

Handle long enough to avoid stooping

Back straight and slightly arched

Feet spaced apart

Weeding & Planting

Hoe rather than hand pull weeds if you are over 50 and/or suffer from back trouble

Don't stoop or bend – kneel on a soft mat. Sit on a low stool instead of kneeling if your knees are arthritic

Keep close to the plant – don't stretch too far forward or sideways

Digging & Forking

Back straight and slightly arched

Handle long enough to avoid stooping

Let your legs do the work rather than your back

Flower colours

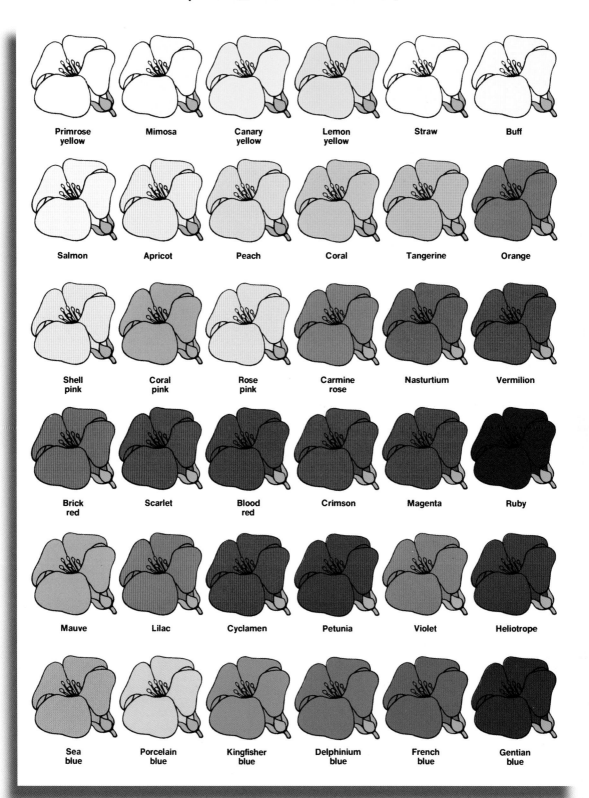

Primrose yellow	**Mimosa**	**Canary yellow**
Lemon yellow	**Straw**	**Buff**
Salmon	**Apricot**	**Peach**
Coral	**Tangerine**	**Orange**
Shell pink	**Coral pink**	**Rose pink**
Carmine rose	**Nasturtium**	**Vermilion**
Brick red	**Scarlet**	**Blood red**
Crimson	**Magenta**	**Ruby**
Mauve	**Lilac**	**Cyclamen**
Petunia	**Violet**	**Heliotrope**
Sea blue	**Porcelain blue**	**Kingfisher blue**
Delphinium blue	**French blue**	**Gentian blue**

Dealing with rot

The fungus which causes softwood to rot requires both air and a high moisture content. The high risk areas are the parts of the building which are the last to dry out — the bottom of the window frames, the bearers below the floor and the lowest planks of the side walls.

The cardinal rule is that prevention is much easier than trying to cure the problem. New wood should be either naturally resistant to the fungus or it should be protected against rot by having had preservative forced inside the grain and not merely painted on the surface. With softwoods you have two choices — you can either treat the surface with a preservative every couple of years or you can paint it at intervals to maintain a waterproof coating.

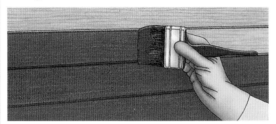

Preservative rules first. Choose with care — creosote has its followers but tends to be messy and smelly. Best of all are the modern water-based preservatives which form a waterproof but breathing film over the surface — check that a fungicide is present. Scrub down the walls, doors etc and allow to dry thoroughly before treatment. Choose a dry day and apply the preservative liberally with a brush. Pay particular attention to cut ends of timber and begin work at the bottom and progress steadily up to the roof.

With paint you should carry out all necessary repairs before you begin — replacing rotten wood, reglazing broken windows etc. Choose a settled spell and rub down the surface with glass paper after filling cracks and holes. Work from the top downwards.

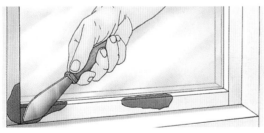

Unfortunately, rot may already be present. Test with a small screwdriver or steel point — rotten wood is soft. If only a small area is affected, use a wood repair kit. Cut away the rotten area and paint with hardener to strengthen the timber. After about 6 hours restore the original level with the wood filler. Insert the preservative tablets into the surrounding sound wood.

This technique is obviously better suited to painted than stained surfaces. With stained wood it may be better to cut out rotten areas and replace with sound timber — this course of action has to be taken in any case if the area of rot is extensive.

Name that shrub

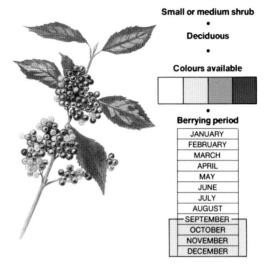

Small or medium shrub

•

Deciduous

•

Colours available

•

Berrying period

| JANUARY |
| FEBRUARY |
| MARCH |
| APRIL |
| MAY |
| JUNE |
| JULY |
| AUGUST |
| SEPTEMBER |
| OCTOBER |
| NOVEMBER |
| DECEMBER |

The beauty of this shrub is seen in the autumn. The leaves will have turned rose, violet or red and when they fall the polished berries are revealed on the bare stems. The outstanding feature is that these fruits are not the common-or-garden red or black we usually associate with shrub berries — they are lilac, violet or bright purple. The colourful clusters persist until Christmas. Plant the bushes in groups rather than singly to make sure that berries will be plentiful — cut branches are excellent for winter flower arranging.

Answer on page 128

The garden seasons

DECEMBER	
JANUARY	Winter
FEBRUARY	
MARCH	
APRIL	Spring
MAY	
JUNE	
JULY	Summer
AUGUST	
SEPTEMBER	
OCTOBER	Autumn
NOVEMBER	

The growing season

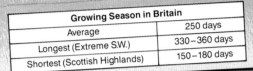

STARTS when the soil temperature reaches 6°C ▼

The **Growing Season** is the period of the year when most plants (including grass) are in growth. This growth may be slow at the start and finish of the growing season, and may cease altogether if there is an unseasonal frost.

FINISHES when the soil temperature falls below 6°C ▼

Growing Season in Britain	
Average	250 days
Longest (Extreme S.W.)	330–360 days
Shortest (Scottish Highlands)	150–180 days

Digging

Dig only if the soil is in bad condition. When digging it is essential to put a layer of organic matter at the bottom of the trench before turning over the soil to fill it. This trench must never be deep enough to bring up a subsoil of clay, chalk or sand.

(1) Choose the right season — early winter for most soils and early spring for light land. Choose the right day — the ground should be moist but not water-logged nor frozen

(2) Wear clothes that are warm — you should not be uncomfortably hot nor cold when digging. Make sure your back is fully covered and wear stout shoes

(3) Use the right equipment — a spade for general work or a fork if the soil is very heavy or stony. Carry a scraper and use it to keep the blade or prongs clean

(4) Try to keep your back straight — avoid any sudden twists from the hips and on no account strain harder than you are used to doing at home or at work

(5)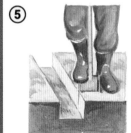

Drive in the spade vertically. Press (do not kick) down on the blade. This should be at right angles to the trench

(6)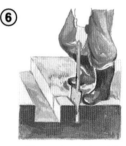

The next cut should be parallel to the trench, 6–8 in. (15–20 cm) behind the face. Do not take larger slices

(7)

Pull steadily (do not jerk) on the handle so as to lever the soil on to the blade. Lift up the block of soil

(8)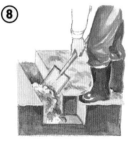

With a flick of the wrist turn the earth into the trench in front — turn the spadeful right over to bury the weeds

(9) Work for 10 minutes if you are reasonably fit but out of condition, then sit down or do a non-strenuous job until you feel rested. Work for 20 minutes between rests if you are fit and used to physical exercise. For most people 30 minutes digging is quite enough for the first day

Large Areas

Think twice before lifting a spade if you have a large area of hard and compacted earth to turn over. A typical example is the ground left by the builders. Hire a cultivator which can work to a depth of 8 in. (20 cm) or call in a contractor.

Rabbits

A serious problem in rural areas. Flowers, shrubs and vegetables are nibbled and bark may be gnawed. There is no easy answer. Tree guards will protect individual woody plants, but deterrents soon lose their power and ordinary fences are ineffective. A rabbit fence uses 1.5 m wire netting with the bottom 30 cm buried below ground. They can be shot, trapped or gassed, but many people find this distasteful and it rarely fully solves the problem. Lists of 'resistant' plants are not always reliable.

Anatomy of a rose

Number of Petals

SINGLE	SEMI-DOUBLE	DOUBLE		
less than 8 petals	8-20 petals	MODERATELY FULL 21-29 petals	FULL 30-39 petals	VERY FULL 40 petals and over
Examples: Ballerina Dortmund Fred Loads Mermaid	Examples: Boy's Brigade Joseph's Coat Masquerade Sweet Magic	Example: Pascali	Example: Dearest	Example: Peace

Petal Shapes

The petals of many roses are **plain**, but those of Hybrid Teas and some Floribundas are **reflexed**. A feature of a few roses is a wavy or **ruffled** edge to the petals, and in the *Grootendorst* varieties the petals have a carnation-like **frilled** edge.

PLAIN
Example: Nevada

REFLEXED
Example: Alec's Red

RUFFLED
Example: Just Joey

FRILLED
Example: F. J. Grootendorst

Flower Shapes

HIGH-CENTRED
Classical shape of the Hybrid Tea – long inner petals forming a regular central cone.

SPLIT-CENTRED
Inner petals confused, forming an irregular central area.

BLOWN
Normally well-shaped bloom past its best – opened wide to reveal stamens.

GLOBULAR
Bloom possessing many petals forming a ball-like arrangement with a closed centre.

OPEN-CUPPED
Bloom possessing many petals forming a cup-like arrangement with an open centre.

QUARTERED
Inner petals folded into 4 distinct sections rather than forming a cone.

FLAT
Flat, low-centred bloom with a small number of petals.

ROSETTE
Flat, low-centred bloom with many short petals regularly arranged.

POMPON
Rounded bloom with many short petals regularly arranged.

Fruit tree dictionary

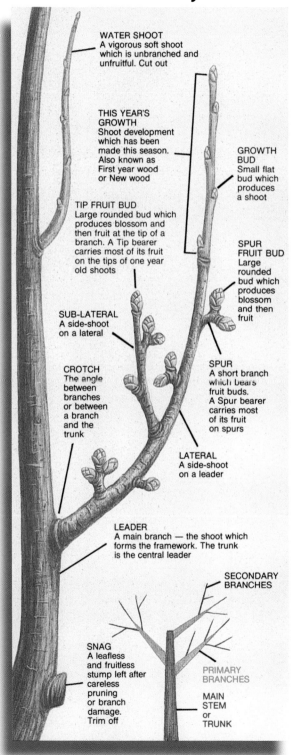

WATER SHOOT
A vigorous soft shoot which is unbranched and unfruitful. Cut out

THIS YEAR'S GROWTH
Shoot development which has been made this season. Also known as First year wood or New wood

GROWTH BUD
Small flat bud which produces a shoot

TIP FRUIT BUD
Large rounded bud which produces blossom and then fruit at the tip of a branch. A Tip bearer carries most of its fruit on the tips of one year old shoots

SPUR FRUIT BUD
Large rounded bud which produces blossom and then fruit

SUB-LATERAL
A side-shoot on a lateral

CROTCH
The angle between branches or between a branch and the trunk

SPUR
A short branch which bears fruit buds. A Spur bearer carries most of its fruit on spurs

LATERAL
A side-shoot on a leader

LEADER
A main branch — the shoot which forms the framework. The trunk is the central leader

SECONDARY BRANCHES

SNAG
A leafless and fruitless stump left after careless pruning or branch damage. Trim off

PRIMARY BRANCHES

MAIN STEM or TRUNK

> "You can get off alcohol, drugs, women, food and cars, but once you're hooked on orchids you are finished. You never get off orchids. Never."
> *Orchid Fever* (Eric Hansen)

Hiring equipment

There may be times when there is a job to do which calls for heavier and more expensive equipment than you have in the tool shed. If the task is a regular one such as cutting a large lawn then you should consider buying a larger mower, or if there are many trees to prune then you should certainly buy long-handled pruners to complement the secateurs. Some big jobs, however, are one-offs — moving a large amount of rubbish, cutting an extensive area of over-grown grass, cutting down a number of trees, turning over an uncultivated plot etc. Hiring the necessary equipment is the answer.

- When hiring, be clear about what you want. Cement mixers, mowers, cultivators, skips, chainsaws, hedge trimmers, conveyors etc come in a range of sizes
- Look at the equipment carefully. Check for loose nuts, missing parts, frayed cables and so on
- Obtain instructions — get a manual if possible or carefully write down what has to be done. Ask for a demonstration if practical
- Make sure that you have the necessary safety equipment
- Look at the contract before signing. Make sure the item is in good condition if that is how it is described

Pot plant danger signs

DANGER SIGNS: TOO LITTLE WATER

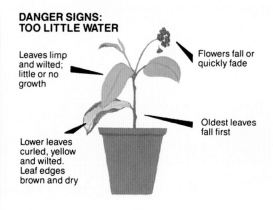

Leaves limp and wilted; little or no growth

Flowers fall or quickly fade

Oldest leaves fall first

Lower leaves curled, yellow and wilted. Leaf edges brown and dry

DANGER SIGNS: TOO MUCH WATER

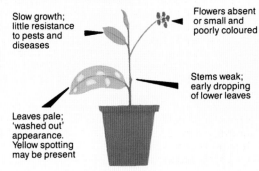

Flowers mouldy

Leaves limp; soft, rotten areas. Poor growth

Both young and old leaves fall at the same time

Leaves curled, yellow and wilted. Leaf tips brown

Roots brown and mushy

DANGER SIGNS: TEMPERATURE IS WRONG

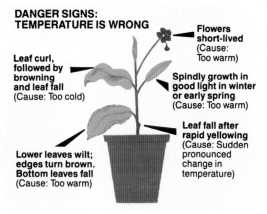

Flowers short-lived (Cause: Too warm)

Leaf curl, followed by browning and leaf fall (Cause: Too cold)

Spindly growth in good light in winter or early spring (Cause: Too warm)

Leaf fall after rapid yellowing (Cause: Sudden pronounced change in temperature)

Lower leaves wilt; edges turn brown. Bottom leaves fall (Cause: Too warm)

DANGER SIGNS: TOO LITTLE FERTILIZER

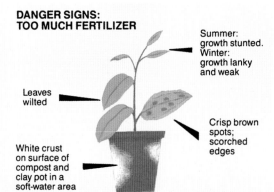

Slow growth; little resistance to pests and diseases

Flowers absent or small and poorly coloured

Stems weak; early dropping of lower leaves

Leaves pale; 'washed out' appearance. Yellow spotting may be present

DANGER SIGNS: TOO LITTLE LIGHT

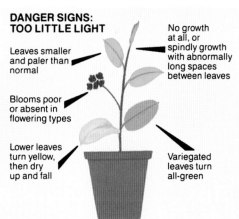

Leaves smaller and paler than normal

No growth at all, or spindly growth with abnormally long spaces between leaves

Blooms poor or absent in flowering types

Lower leaves turn yellow, then dry up and fall

Variegated leaves turn all-green

DANGER SIGNS: TOO MUCH FERTILIZER

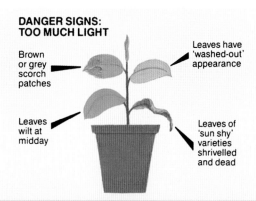

Summer: growth stunted. Winter: growth lanky and weak

Leaves wilted

Crisp brown spots; scorched edges

White crust on surface of compost and clay pot in a soft-water area

DANGER SIGNS: TOO MUCH LIGHT

Brown or grey scorch patches

Leaves have 'washed-out' appearance

Leaves wilt at midday

Leaves of 'sun shy' varieties shrivelled and dead

Frog or toad?

COMMON FROG

8 cm long. Various skin colours, marbled black or brown

- Smooth, moist skin, angular body
- Dark marking behind the eye
- Moves in a series of leaps, up to 50 cm in length
- Tadpoles have a pointed tip, long and powerful hind legs

COMMON TOAD

10 cm long. Skin colour brown, olive or grey

- Warty, dry skin, squat, rounded body
- No dark marking behind the eye
- Moves with a clumsy, ambling gait. Hops are very feeble
- Tadpoles have a rounded tip, hind legs shorter and less powerful

In early spring frogs and toads move to ponds where mating takes place. In May–June tadpoles emerge from the spawn. In July the tiny frogs and toads move on to the land – in October they hibernate.

Growing vegetables in beds

FLAT BEDS

The flat bed is the easiest type to create but you do need free-draining soil. Use the dimensions given for raised beds in the drawing below. Turn over the soil and work in a 1 in. (2.5 cm) layer of organic material.

RAISED BEDS

10 ft (3 m) maximum

2-3 ft (60-90 cm)

4 ft (1.2 m)

1½ ft (45 cm)

Pathway covered with gravel or coarse bark chippings. Put black plastic sheeting underneath to prevent weed growth

The raised bed is the type to create if drainage is poor and the ground gets waterlogged in winter. You will have to build retaining walls — see the drawing above. Railway sleepers, bricks or blocks can be used but 1 in. (2.5 cm) thick pressure-treated wooden planks attached to 2 in. (5 cm) square corner posts are the usual choice. The raised bed should be at least 4 in. (10 cm) high — fork over the bottom and then fill with a mixture of 2 parts topsoil and 1 part organic matter.

Layering

Some small shrubs such as Lavender, Vinca and Ceratostigma form clumps which can be split up like hardy perennials and the pieces replanted, but shrub propagation nearly always leaves the parent plant undisturbed. Shrubs with flexible stems can be raised very easily by layering — some plants (e.g Rhododendron and Magnolia) produce new plants naturally by this method. To layer a shrub or climber, a stem is pegged down in spring or autumn and left attached to the parent plant until roots have formed at the base of the layered shoot. This takes 6-12 months. Suitable subjects include Berberis, Camellia, Clematis, Forsythia, Heather, Japonica, Lilac, Lonicera, Magnolia and Rhododendron.

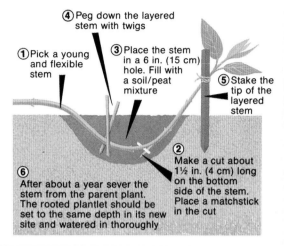

④ Peg down the layered stem with twigs

① Pick a young and flexible stem

③ Place the stem in a 6 in. (15 cm) hole. Fill with a soil/peat mixture

⑤ Stake the tip of the layered stem

② Make a cut about 1½ in. (4 cm) long on the bottom side of the stem. Place a matchstick in the cut

⑥ After about a year sever the stem from the parent plant. The rooted plantlet should be set to the same depth in its new site and watered in thoroughly

Rogues gallery

SLUGS & SNAILS

Generally regarded as enemy No.1 in the garden, especially when the weather is wet and cool. They are not usually seen during the day, so look for the tell-tale slime trails. Young plants are particularly susceptible and may be killed — the leaves of lettuce, brassicas, celery etc are holed and stems are damaged. The ragged edges of affected leaves are susceptible to attack by the grey mould fungus. Potato tubers may be riddled by the underground **keeled slug**. Keep the surrounding area free from rubbish. The standard method of control is to scatter slug pellets thinly around the plants at the first sign of attack. Non-chemical methods of killing or deterring slugs and snails are using traps filled with beer, placing a ring of gritty sand around individual plants, and applying slug-killing nematodes to the soil. On heavy land avoid planting slug-susceptible potato varieties such as Cara and Maris Piper.

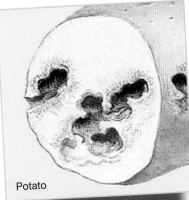

Lettuce

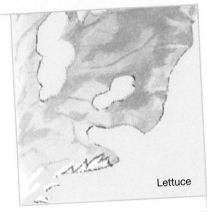

Potato

When to prune

The following table is a general guide to pruning. There are a number of exceptions and the rule to follow is that if you are in doubt — don't prune.

DECIDUOUS SHRUBS WHICH BLOOM BEFORE THE END OF MAY

Time: As soon as flowering is over — do not delay

Cut out all weak, dead and awkwardly-placed shoots and then remove overcrowded or invasive branches.

Flowers are produced on old wood. Some of the branches which have borne flowers should therefore be cut back — new, vigorous growth will develop and this will bear flowers next season.

DECIDUOUS SHRUBS WHICH BLOOM AFTER THE END OF MAY

Time: January-March — do not wait until growth starts

Cut out all weak, dead and awkwardly-placed shoots and then remove overcrowded or invasive branches.

Flowers are produced on new wood. If flowering has been poor cut back some of the old branches to stimulate fresh growth for next year's flowers.

FLOWERING CHERRIES & CONIFERS

Time: Late summer or autumn — never in winter

Cut out all dead wood and overcrowded or invasive branches.

EVERGREEN SHRUBS

Time: May

Cut out all weak, dead and awkwardly-placed shoots and then remove overcrowded or invasive stems. With some of these plants (Santolina, Rhododendron, Buxus etc) hard pruning can be used to regenerate bushes with leggy stems.

HEDGES

Time: See page 84. Trim an informal flowering hedge when blooms have faded

The established formal hedge should be kept at 4-6 ft (1.2-1.8 m) and the top should be narrower than the base. You can use shears but an electric hedgetrimmer will save time. Place plastic sheeting at the base of the hedge — this will make clipping removal much easier.

Fruiting shrubs

Akebia species
Amelancher species
Arbutus species
Arctostaphylos species
Aucuba species
Callicarpa species
Chaenomeles species
Clerodendrum species
Cornus species
Corylus species
Cotoneaster species
Crataegus species
Daphne species
Decaisnea species
Euonymus species
Fatsia species
Gaultheria species
Hippophae species
Hypericum species
Ilex species
Jasminum beesianum
Leycesteria species
Lonicera species
Mahonia species
Myrica species
Myrtus species
Pernettya species
Prunus species
Pyracantha species
Ribes species
Rosa species
Rubus species
Sambucus species
Sarcococca species
Skimmia species
Solarium species
Sorbus species
Stranvaesia species
Symphoricarpos species
Vaccinium species
Viburnum species

Using the grass box

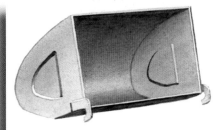

There is a temptation to leave clippings on the lawn — nutrients are returned to the soil, drought resistance is improved, moss is inhibited and you are saved the chore of taking the clippings away.

In most cases, however, the disadvantages far outweigh the advantages. Weeds are spread, the turf becomes spongy and susceptible to disease, worm activity is greatly encouraged and aeration is impeded.

The general rule is to remove grass clippings each time you mow, but if the weather is hot and dry and if the turf is reasonably weed-free, leave the clippings on the lawn to cut down water loss from the surface.

Crocus types

DUTCH HYBRIDS

C. 'Pickwick'

CHRYSANTHUS HYBRIDS

C. 'Cream Beauty'

SPRING-FLOWERING SPECIES

C. tommasinianus

AUTUMN-FLOWERING SPECIES

C. speciosus

Greenhouse types

COLD GREENHOUSE
Unheated except by the sun

**minimum temperature -2° C
when outside temperature falls to -7° C**

COOL GREENHOUSE
Heater required during the cooler months

minimum temperature 7° C

WARM GREENHOUSE
Heater required during most months

minimum temperature 13° C

Cast-iron house plants

Zebrina

Chlorophytum

There is a group of plants which will tolerate an amazing range of conditions — dreary and cold corners, bright and stuffy rooms, periods of neglect and so on. Grow some of these plants if you are convinced that everything you touch will die. These plants won't, providing you don't keep the compost saturated and you don't bake them on an unshaded south-facing windowsill in summer. Watering should really be based on the particular needs of each plant, but as a general rule you can water once a week during the growing season and once every two weeks in winter.

Asparagus	Fatshedera	Pothos
Aspidistra	Fatsia	Sansevieria
Billbergia	Helxine	Succulents
Chlorophytum	Monstera	Tradescantia
Cissus	Parlour Palm	Zebrina

Trees and subsidence

Tree roots close to the foundations of a house can cause subsidence during a prolonged drought. The situation is most likely to occur in clayey soil areas. The uptake of water by the roots hastens soil shrinkage, the foundations crack and this results in cracks along the house wall. Listed below are the safe minimum distances between various trees and a house wall. Obviously the best plan is to meet this requirement at planting time, but you may already have a tall tree very close to the house. It is tempting to cut it down straight away, but take care. It may be covered by a Tree Preservation Order, and it is unwise to think of instant removal. This could result in heave, the opposite of subsidence and just as damaging. This is caused by an excess of water in the soil which used to be taken up by the tree roots. The answer is to bring the tree under control by cutting back over a number of years.

Safe distance between tree trunk and house wall

5 m	10 m	20 m	30 m	40 m
Holly	Apple, Pear	Ash	Horse Chestnut	Poplar
Laurel	Birch	Beech	Lime	Willow
Yew	Cherry	C. leylandii	Oak	
	Hawthorn	Gum tree		
	Laburnum	Maple		
	Mountain Ash	Plane		
	Pine	Sycamore		

Anatomy of a patio

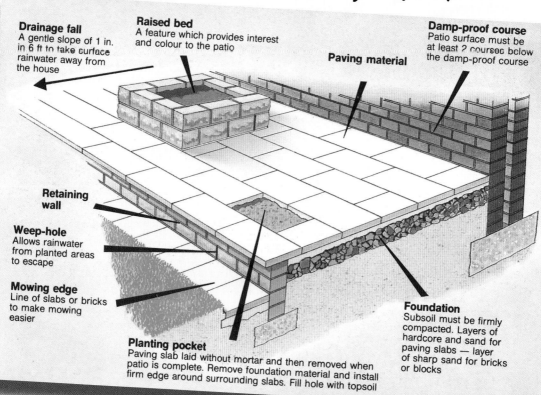

Drainage fall
A gentle slope of 1 in. in 6 ft to take surface rainwater away from the house

Raised bed
A feature which provides interest and colour to the patio

Damp-proof course
Patio surface must be at least 2 courses below the damp-proof course

Paving material

Retaining wall

Weep-hole
Allows rainwater from planted areas to escape

Mowing edge
Line of slabs or bricks to make mowing easier

Planting pocket
Paving slab laid without mortar and then removed when patio is complete. Remove foundation material and install firm edge around surrounding slabs. Fill hole with topsoil

Foundation
Subsoil must be firmly compacted. Layers of hardcore and sand for paving slabs — layer of sharp sand for bricks or blocks

Flower arranging styles : 2

The LINE Style

Open space within the boundary of the arrangement is a key feature. The Line style is the opposite of the Mass design (page 20) in nearly every way. Origin, mechanics and the choice and use of plant material are all quite different. The Line concept originated in the East and rules were laid down in China more than 1000 years ago — the Mass style is a product of the West and began much later. The basic feature of a Line design is limited use of plant material with support often provided by a pinholder — in the traditional Mass arrangement there are lots of flowers and/or foliage supported in either floral foam or crumpled chicken wire.

These are perhaps details — the fundamental feature of the Line style is that each element of the design is important in its own right and the air space contained within the framing line material is vital to the overall effect of the display. As the name indicates, it is the lines and not the mass which are the main source of appeal. Another key difference is that a gradual change in colour and shape between neighbouring plants is not important — in fact it is positively undesirable with many Line arrangements. We do not know just when the Line style was adopted in the West — Ikebana aroused much interest when exhibited at the first Chelsea Flower Show in 1912, but it was in the U.S between 1955 and 1975 that the Western Line style really took hold.

Name that flower

Summer bedding plant
•
Half hardy annual
•
Colours available
•
Flowering period

| JANUARY |
| FEBRUARY |
| MARCH |
| APRIL |
| MAY |
| JUNE |
| JULY |
| AUGUST |
| SEPTEMBER |
| OCTOBER |
| NOVEMBER |
| DECEMBER |

Plant one as a centrepiece in a formal bedding scheme or in a large container. During the summer the 1½ ft (45 cm) long tassels of tiny blooms are a spectacular feature which can be used fresh or dried in flower arrangements. Keep the plants watered during dry spells to prolong the flowering period and to ensure an attractive autumn display of red stems and bronzy leaves. Support the stems with twigs if the site is exposed.

Answer on page 128

Dead-heading

The removal of dead flowers has several advantages — it helps to keep the bed or border tidy, it prolongs the flowering seasons by preventing seed formation and in a few cases (e.g Lupin and Delphinium) it induces a second flush later in the season.

Use garden shears, secateurs, a sharp knife or finger tips depending on the type of plant. Be careful not to remove too much stem. You must not dead-head flowers grown for their seed pods (Honesty, Chinese Lantern etc).

It is quite impractical to remove the dead blooms from some annuals and perennials and from most trees and shrubs. There are a few large-flowering woody plants, however, which must be dead-headed. The faded trusses of Hybrid Tea and Floribunda Roses should be cut off and the dead flowers of Rhododendrons should be carefully broken off with finger and thumb. Cut off the flower-heads of Lilac once the blooms have faded, but the large heads of Hydrangeas are an exception — remove in March.

Repairing cracks

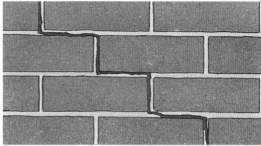

Non-serious cracking is illustrated above. The crack follows a zig-zag path through the mortar and may extend for several courses. Apart from the crack the wall remains firm and vertical, and in this case remedial action is fairly simple. All you have to do is to rake out the damaged mortar in the affected area and then repoint as described on page 111. You should soak the bricks thoroughly before repointing and take care to push the mortar deeply into the space between the courses. If the cracking occurs at the top of the wall it is generally more satisfactory to remove the bricks involved and relay them as illustrated on page 77. The problem of matching the surrounding mortar colour is the only difficult feature of repairing non-serious cracks — see the Repointing section on page 111 for advice.

A key feature of serious cracking is that bricks as well as the mortar are split and the crack generally runs vertically. It may be that the wall has received a heavy blow or that the mortar used was far too wet, but the usual cause is subsidence. This occurs when the foundations move downwards — upwards movement is called heave. The reason may be that the base was improperly laid — but even a properly-laid foundation can move on heavy clay which has been subjected to very wet winters and very dry summers.

If the serious cracking has caused the wall to lean or become unstable then the only course of action is to pull the wall down and rebuild. Do this immediately or rope off the area if the damaged wall is a danger to passers-by. Provided the wall is vertical and firm, the next step is to determine whether the crack is widening. This calls for the glass slide test illustrated above. Glue a thin glass slide over the crack. If the glass breaks within a few weeks then the problem is progressively getting worse — the only course of action is to demolish the wall and start again. Only if the wall is vertical, firm and with cracks which are not widening should you attempt to repair the damage by simple repointing.

Moss control

Small patches of moss are not a problem, but large mossy areas are unsightly. Unfortunately there is no easy solution. The not-so-green gardener can burn it off with lawn sand, but this offers only short-term relief. If you don't remove the basic cause or causes then the moss will return. Poor drainage is an important culprit, so making holes with a fork in a mossy patch on compacted soil will help. Other causes are shade, lack of nutrients in sandy soil and over-acidity (lime will help, but do test first). The best advice is to apply a fertilizer in spring, spike the affected areas in autumn, remove the cause of shade if possible, top dress, and always cut at the recommended height – closely shaving the lawn is a common cause of moss infestation.

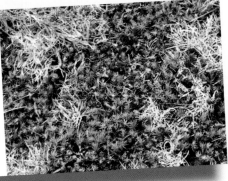

Mowing calendar

START

Begin in **March** or **early April**, depending on the locality and the weather. It is time for the first cut when the soil is reasonably dry and the grass is starting to grow actively. With this first cut set the blades high so that the grass is merely tipped, not shorn.

MARCH

MOW REGULARLY

As a general rule the cutting height should be 2.5 cm and mowing should take place at weekly intervals. However, there are several exceptions to this standard procedure:

- Set the blades at 3-4 cm for the first couple of cuts in spring and for the last few cuts in autumn.
- Set the blades at 4 cm during periods of prolonged drought if the lawn is not being regularly watered. The longer grass will help to cut down water loss.
- Cut at fortnightly rather than weekly intervals if the grass is growing very slowly – for example under trees or during prolonged drought.
- If you have had to be away for a couple of weeks or more in summer then merely tip it at the first cut following your return. Reduce the height at the next cut and then continue with 2.5 cm high cuts.

APRIL

MAY

JUNE

JULY

AUGUST

SEPTEMBER

FINISH

Stop in **October** when the growth of the grass has slowed right down and the soil has become very moist. Put the mower away, but rake off fallen leaves on the surface of the lawn. Keen gardeners lightly 'top' the grass occasionally in winter when the weather is mild, but it is not essential. Avoid walking on the lawn when it is frozen or covered in snow.

OCTOBER

House plant design terms

HUE, TINT & SHADE

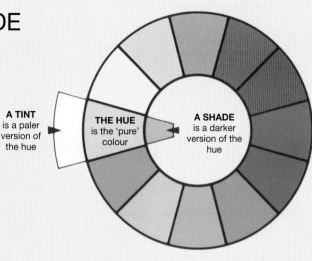

THE WARM COLOURS
The warm colours brighten up the display. The hues are often dramatic and direct the eye away from the cool colours — the tints and shades are more subdued.

WHITE
White on its own has a calming effect — when placed next to warm colours the result is to make them look brighter.

THE COOL COLOURS
The cool colours quieten down the display. The hues are restful and provide an air of tranquility, but they are overshadowed by bright warm colours.

A TINT is a paler version of the hue

THE HUE is the 'pure' colour

A SHADE is a darker version of the hue

MONOCHROMATIC DISPLAY
In a monochromatic scheme the various tints and shades of a single hue are the colours of the flowers and/or the non-green parts of the leaves.

ANALOGOUS DISPLAY
In an analogous scheme the two, three or four hues of the flowers and/or the non-green parts of the leaves are all neighbours on the colour wheel.

CONTRASTING DISPLAY
In a contrasting scheme the two hues of the flowers and/or the non-green parts of the leaves are directly opposite on the colour wheel.

POLYCHROMATIC DISPLAY
In a polychromatic (or rainbow) scheme the hues of the flowers and/or the non-green parts of the leaves are from all parts of the wheel.

French bean types

Most french beans are **Bush** varieties, growing as compact branching plants 12-18 in. high. There are a few **Climbing** varieties which will clamber up a support to a height of 5 ft or more. The usual pod colour is green, but you can also buy yellow and purple varieties — there is even a striped one for the novelty seeker. The coloured pod has a practical advantage — the pods can be easily seen at picking time.

FLAT-POD varieties (F)
Before the War these varieties dominated the catalogues. They are the 'English' varieties — flat, rather wide and often with a tendency to become stringy as they mature. You will find the old favourites here, but there are some new stringless varieties such as Limelight.

PENCIL-POD varieties (P)
The catalogues are now dominated by those 'Continental' varieties — round and generally stringless. Small pods are usually cooked whole.

French beans are nearly always eaten in the fresh green pod state — the 'haricot vert' of the French. With some varieties (Chevrier Vert is the notable example) the fresh bean ('flageolet') can be removed from the pods and cooked, or dried ('haricot') for cooking later.

Not for eating

Scores of garden plants can cause stomach upsets and other undesirable effects when the berries, seeds or other parts are swallowed. Nearly 2000 children go to hospital each year for observation and occasionally for treatment, and so the danger must be taken seriously. But don't panic — fatalities are very rare. Seek medical treatment promptly if any part of a plant listed below has been eaten — take along the plant if you can and a sample of vomit if the patient has been sick.

Box (leaves)
Bryony (any part)
Cherry laurel (berries)
Cotoneaster (berries)
Daphne (any part)
Datura (seeds)
Deadly nightshade (any part)

Dieffenbachia (stems)
Foxglove (berries & leaves)
Hellebore (any part)
Holly (berries)
Ivy (berries)
Juniper (berries)
Laburnum (pods)

Lords & ladies (berries)
Mistletoe (berries)
Privet (berries & leaves)
Spindle (berries & leaves)
Sweet pea (berries)
Winter cherry (berries)
Yew (berries)

Taxus baccata (Yew)

Laburnum anagyroides (Laburnum)

Daphne mezereum (Daphne)

Euonymus europaeus (Spindle)

Ligustrum vulgare (Privet)

... and not for touching

Much less has been written about plant allergies than plant poisoning, but they are much more common and are less easy to avoid. About one in every 5 gardeners is affected at some time. It is wise to wear gloves when handling any of the plants below if you have suffered from a rash, itching or swollen patches on the skin after gardening. Do be especially careful with the plants which cause hypersensitivity to sunlight (marked * below). The sap in the leaves can induce sunburn without prolonged exposure to sunlight.

Bamboo (stems & leaves)
Borage (leaves)
Bugloss (leaves)
Bulbs (sap)
*Carrot (leaves)
*Celery (leaves)
Chrysanthemum (stems & leaves)

Cucumber (stems & leaves)
Daphne (leaves)
Geranium (leaves)
Hellebore (sap)
Marrow (stems & leaves)
Nettle (stems & leaves)
*Parsnip (leaves)

Poinsettia (sap)
Primula (leaves)
Radish (leaves)
Rhus (leaves)
*Rue (leaves & sap)
Strawberry (leaves)
Tomato (leaves)

* Plants which cause hypersensitivity to sunlight

Primula obconica (Poison Primrose)

Crysanthemum hybrid (Crysanthemum)

Rhus typhina (Sumach)

Pelargonium hortorum (Geranium)

Raphanus sativus (Radish)

Pots

STANDARD PLANT POT

This is the most popular free-standing container available in many sizes and several different materials. The basic shape is square or round with gently sloping sides and the basic materials are ordinary clay, high quality terra-cotta and inexpensive plastic. It is generally employed where the plant and not the container is the decorative feature and where the amount of plant material is not extensive. It may be rimmed or rimless, glazed or unglazed and with or without a saucer. Choose a **half pot** where a larger compost surface area is required

LONG TOM POT

An old-fashioned type for the back of a group of pots. Useful for trailing plants, but stability can be a problem — not often seen at garden centres

CYLINDRICAL POT

Available in terracotta, plastic and reconstituted stone. Surface may be moulded — e.g a **cherub pot**. Sometimes called a **chimney pot**

BELL POT

An attractive shape — an upturned bell with a flat base. Both unglazed terracota and glazed earthenware are widely available

GARLAND POT

This type of pot has a decorative surface. The garland of leaves, fruits etc may be simple or complex. Sometimes called a **swag pot**

ORANGE POT

A wide-mouthed pot with a prominent ridge around the body. Once used for displaying Orange trees. Other name — **Roman Vase**

ORIENTAL POT

Many types available — the glazed surface may be muted or colourful and lettering or plant motifs may be an added feature

STANDARD JAR

This differs from a pot by having a restricted neck. Less suitable than a pot for growing plants, but a jar can be a focal point feature, especially where a Mediterranean or Oriental effect is sought

ALI BABA JAR

A popular terracotta jar — the basic features are a strong rim at the top and the widest part is just below the neck. Usually large

CRETAN JAR

The widest part is the centre of the jar — handles may be present. Known as a **beehive jar** when the surface has a series of ridges

WINE JAR

A jar with a narrow base and large handles is often referred to as a wine jar. Here the container itself is the main decorative feature

MULTIPOT

Several terracotta pots fused together — a number of brands are available. Not for the purist, perhaps, but can be eye-catching

VASE

An unusual shape — a flower-vase shaped pot in terracotta with an extended base for stability. Not very practical

Hoeing

The hoe has two important functions. Its main task is to keep weeds under control — hoeing must be carried out at regular intervals to keep annual weeds in check and to starve out the underground parts of perennial weeds. Weeds should be severed just below ground level rather than being dragged to the surface — to ensure success keep the blade sharp at all times. The second important function of hoeing is to break up the surface pan which can be a problem in some soils after rain.

The proper way to use a hoe depends upon the type. With a Dutch hoe you push the blade forward as you walk backwards — the blade is held just below the soil surface. The advantages are the avoidance of walking on the hoed area and the superior weed-cutting action. The draw hoe is used with a chopping rather than a slicing motion — the blade is brought down in short chopping strokes as you walk slowly backwards. There are advantages — it is more effective than a Dutch hoe on hard ground and it is safer for use when working near to plants. Draw hoes have other uses such as earthing up Potatoes and Celery, and the corner of the blade is often used for drawing seed drills.

Hoe with care. Roots of some plants lie close to the surface, and much damage is done by hoeing too deeply. Don't hoe if weeds are absent and the surface is not caked — the 'dust mulch' has now been found to be of no value as a way of cutting down water loss.

Name that shrub

Large shrub
•
Semi-evergreen
or
Evergreen
•
Colour available

•
Flowering period

| JANUARY |
| FEBRUARY |
| MARCH |
| APRIL |
| MAY |
| JUNE |
| JULY |
| AUGUST |
| SEPTEMBER |
| OCTOBER |
| NOVEMBER |
| DECEMBER |

The experts cannot agree whether this American shrub is hardy or not. A few say that it is sensitive to frost and that it will only withstand a milder-than-average winter, but others say that once established it can withstand a severe frost. It does seem to be hardy, but needs the protection from wind which a south-facing wall provides. Nobody argues about its charm — it is a showy shrub which bears large yellow flowers from late spring to mid autumn. It grows quickly, bearing leathery lobed leaves on its down-covered stems — hence the common name. A word of warning — this down can be extremely irritating.

Answer on page 128

Screen planting

A screening plant is a variety which is grown primarily to protect the garden from an undesirable feature such as an unattractive view or the prevailing wind. There are three properties of a successful screening plant — it should be evergreen or semi-evergreen, it must be densely covered with leaves for most purposes (see below) and it must be quick-growing.

The usual way of blocking out an unattractive view is to plant Ilex, Ligustrum or a vigorous conifer such as Chamaecyparis lawsoniana or Cupressocyparis leylandii — do remember when planting tall-growing conifers that if left unchecked they can become a worse nuisance than the unpleasant view.

On exposed sites a line of screening plants is sometimes grown to provide a windbreak. For this purpose the dense growth required for hiding ugly objects or views is no longer a desirable property. A wall of dense foliage causes turbulence — a less solid growth habit absorbs the wind. The width of the wind-protected zone behind the screen is about six times the height. A wide band of screening plants can reduce the noise level from passing traffic but a single line of conifers will do virtually nothing to reduce the problem.

Rogues gallery

LILY BEETLE

The bright red beetles and their 1 cm slime-covered orange grubs should be picked off the leaves when seen — the foliage and flowers of lily, fritillaria and convallaria can be seriously damaged by this pest. Once confined to a few southern counties but it is now more widely spread. Spray with bifenthrin.

The way to mow

1 Zebra stripes, those alternate light and dark bands seen so often on mown lawns, are taken by many people to be a sign of quality. They are nothing of the sort. These bands are the result of the lawn being cut in parallel strips with a mower fitted with a roller, the alternate stripes being mown in opposite directions as shown below. An attractive technique, especially as it helps to mask minor imperfections or colour variations, but it is unsightly if not done accurately and neatly.

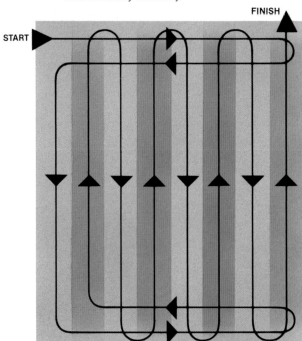

2 Use the correct technique. A mower is not a vacuum cleaner, and is not designed for pushing backwards and forwards as you move along. This push-pull technique is time-wasting with a cylinder mower, risky with a rotary mower and positively dangerous with a hover mower. The correct procedure is to move in a constant forward direction at a steady walking pace. The only exception is when you are manoeuvering in awkward corners.

3 Never leave the machine unattended with the engine running and the cutter blades dis-engaged. Switch off.

4 Electric mowers call for good cable sense. Make sure that the cable is well away from the mower when it is in use, and keep people and pets off the lawn when you are mowing.

5 Wear sensible clothing. If the area is slippery or sloping then stout shoes or boots are a good idea. Never mow in bare feet — such advice should be unnecessary but hospital records show it isn't!

6 Despite the advertising, sloping banks are not child's play for any type of mower. The hover machine is perhaps the best model to use, but you should handle it carefully. Move the mower from side to side in a sweeping semi-circular motion.

7 When using a rotary mower fitted with a grass box, occasionally clean the grass box slots to ensure that the suction system is satisfactory. This is especially important if the grass is wet and long.

8 Never, never make any adjustments while the power is on. However small the problem, however sure and experienced you are, switch off the power before approaching the cutting mechanism.

Miniponds and minipools

There is no precise definition of a minipond — basically it is a miniature pond measuring 1½-4 ft across and is used to cultivate one or more aquatic plants. It may house a few fish but not a fountain — moving water is rarely practical in a tiny pond when plants are present. The fountain and water spout are features of the minipool (see below) rather than the minipond.

There are two reasons for choosing a minipond rather than a regular-sized one. Shortage of space is the usual reason, as a raised minipond can be put on a patio or balcony and both the raised and ground level versions will fit into the smallest garden. The second reason is the undesirability of having a large stretch of water where active and unsupervised toddlers are present.

Any container which will hold at least 5 gallons of water can be used as a minipond as long as it is weatherproof, waterproof, non-corrosive and non-toxic. This rules out copper containers and wooden ones which have contained oil-based products. Half-barrels can be bought from your garden centre — varnish the outside and treat the inside with bitumen paint. Place in a sunny spot and plant with one or more compact Marginals and/or a dwarf Water Lily or two. Depending on the size of your minipond a few Goldfish can be kept, but in a thin-walled raised minipond they will not be happy as water temperature will fluctuate widely during the year. If the pond is very small and you do not have a water heater then move the fish to a larger pond in winter.

The minipool is a reservoir for a moving water feature such as a fountain or water spout. It may be self-contained or custom-built in the garden, and can be placed in sun or shade as there is no plant life to support. The water surface can be covered with pebbles etc, making it perfectly safe for small children.

● **RAISED MINIPOND** An excellent feature for bringing life and interest to the patio. A raised pond made from bricks or blocks can be constructed, but it is more usual to use a ready-made container such as a half-barrel, sink, fibreglass tank or large plastic trough. Lack of insulation against summer heat and winter frost is the main drawback.

● **SURFACE MINIPOND** Any of the containers recommended for a raised minipond can be set into the soil as a surface minipond, but it is more usual to start with a small Rigid or Flexible liner. Compared with the raised version, temperature fluctuation is reduced, but it is still necessary to remove fish in winter if the minipond is very shallow.

● **MINIPOOL** This may be raised or at ground level, and contains neither fish nor plants. It is the ornamental or purely practical catchment area for the water from a fountain or water spout and the water surface may be either uncovered or else concealed by large pebbles. The pebble fountain illustrated on the left has all the virtues of moving water with none of the hazards for toddlers.

Onion types

STANDARD BULB varieties
& JAPANESE BULB varieties

The Standard varieties are grown for their large bulbs which can be stored throughout the winter months. Some have a flattened shape, others are globular. Skin colours vary from almost pure white to bright red and flavours range from mild to strong. Most of them are only suitable for spring sowing but some can be sown in August for a late July crop. The Japanese varieties make late summer sowing a much more reliable routine but their midsummer crop cannot be stored.

SALAD varieties

Thinnings of the Bulb varieties can be used as salad or 'spring' onions, but there are several varieties which are grown specifically for salad use. These Salad varieties, also known as scallions or bunching onions, are white-skinned and mild-flavoured.

PICKLING varieties

Several onion varieties are grown for their small silverskin bulbs (button onions) which are lifted in July or August and picked for use as cocktail onions. These varieties should be sown in April in sandy soil — do not feed. The seedlings should not be thinned.

Dahlia types

Tender perennial
·
**Bedding plant:
half-hardy annual**

**BORDER
DAHLIAS**

**BEDDING
DAHLIAS**

D. 'Yellow Hammer'

**LILLIPUT
DAHLIAS**

D. 'Athalie'

D. 'Little John'

**ANNUAL
DAHLIAS**

D. 'Dandy'

Choosing grass seed

Utility grade

Meadow grass   **Rye grass**

Turf and seed mixtures are made up of broad-leaved grasses with the addition of one or more fine-leaved types such as Chewings Fescue

Luxury grade

Bent   **Fescue**

Turf and seed mixtures are made up of fine-leaved grasses. The broad-leaved grasses are not used, but may appear in mature lawns

Orchid miscellany

Light requirement — nil

The need for bright light for nearly all orchids is stressed many times in this book, but there is an Australian species (**Rhizanthella gardneri**) which lives its life underground in total darkness. The only time it may see daylight is when the autumn flowers occasionally pop up to the surface. Underground insects pollinate the flowers.

It was discovered in 1928 growing in association with the roots of the broom honey myrtle. The pale pink bloom measures ½ in. (1 cm) across.

Raised bedding

It is one of the principles of garden design that a flat and uninteresting plot can be improved by having plants growing at different levels. The rockery and the window box have been used for generations to achieve this effect and more recently both the patio tub and the hanging basket have become popular.

The raised bed is perhaps the most satisfactory way of raising plants above ground level — unlike the container it is truly part of the garden and it can be large enough to provide an impressive display of bedding plants.

A number of walling materials are available — choose the one which is most in keeping with the setting. It should be attractive in its own right or you should plan to cover it with trailing plants. Choose a spot away from trees and draw a plan. The area should not be too large — you must be able to reach the centre without having to climb on to the wall. The height is up to you, but 3 ft (90 cm) is generally considered to be the maximum. The walls must be firm, especially if a large amount of soil is to be retained. A concrete foundation is needed for brick, concrete or stone — sink part of the bottom course below ground level. Wooden walling material must be treated with a preservative and should be firmly embedded into the soil.

When the walling is complete, break up the soil at the bottom of the bed and add a layer of bricks or rubble. Cover with peat or old growing bag compost and then fill with good-quality garden soil. Wait a couple of weeks before planting. The area around the bed should be paved if it joins the lawn — grass growing against a wall is difficult to trim.

Brick

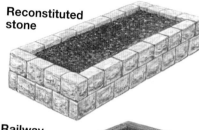

Reconstituted stone

Railway sleepers

Rustic poles

Many types of walling material are suitable — stone, brick, concrete blocks, railway sleepers, peat blocks, reconstituted stone blocks, rustic poles, stout timber boards and pre-cast concrete sections

Stagger rectangular blocks to increase stability

The wall face can be planted with rockery perennials if dry walling (no mortar between stones) or peat blocks are used. Plant as you go when building the wall

The advantages of Raised Bedding

- Small and dainty plants are much easier to see and the perfume of fragrant ones is more noticeable. Miniature Roses and bedded-out house plants take on a new dimension.
- Planting, weeding and dead-heading are easier to do — very important if you are elderly or disabled.
- Drainage is improved — plant roots can be kept away from the high water table in clay soil.
- The area is contained — weeds can't creep in from the surrounding area and the bedding plants can't creep out.
- Attractive pendant plants can be grown to hang over the edge, adding another design element to the bed.
- Children and dogs do not run over the surface — a problem which can occur with surface beds.

Cleaning walls

Bulbs at Xmas

There are several steps involved in cleaning brick and stone walls. Where a covering of white powder is the problem, follow the instructions in the Efflorescence section on page 82. The usual trouble is a combination of dirt, moss and green slime (algae). Begin by using a stiff brush to remove the dirt and surface growths. Next, scrub with plain water — never use soap or detergent. Where moss, algae and mould are present you should use a proprietary moss killer and fungicide. Alternatively you can apply household bleach (1 part bleach : 4 parts water) — leave for about a couple of days and then wash off with plain water. A word of warning — wear goggles when using an anti-slime solution. This chemical treatment will clean the wall but will not solve the basic problem — moss and algae usually indicate excessive dampness, and this must be tackled or the trouble will return.

To renovate brickwork, rub the surface with a piece of similar brick. Stone should be treated with a stone 'sanding block' in the same way — keep the block wet at all times. Mortar as well as masonry may be discoloured — use a proprietary acid-based stone cleaner.

It is not difficult to grow Hyacinths, Narcissi and Tulips for blooming on Christmas Day, but it is not a matter of planting the bulbs earlier than the recommended time. The essential step is to buy bulbs which have been specially treated — look for the word 'prepared' on the label or catalogue entry. These bulbs are more expensive than ordinary garden types and they must be planted as soon as possible after purchase. September is the usual time for planting, and the forcing technique should be followed. Bring the pots indoors when the shoots are 1 in. (2.5 cm) high — this should be no later than the first day of December. After flowering the bulbs can be stored for planting outdoors in autumn.

Anatomy of an indoor trough

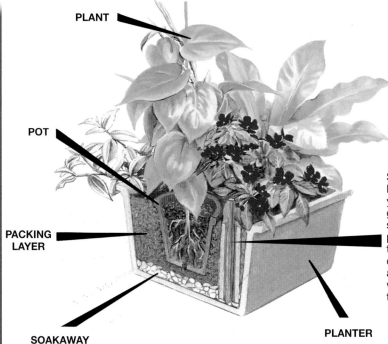

PLANT

POT

PACKING LAYER

SOAKAWAY

PLANTER

WATER GAUGE
Self-watering troughs with water-level indicators are available, but you can build your own water gauge. Insert a tube through the soakaway layer before adding the packing layer — the base of the tube should touch the bottom of the container. Insert a stick in the tube and use it as a dipstick — the water level should not reach above the top of the soakaway.

Surfacing materials

BRICKS & BLOCKS		No heavy lifting is necessary. Bricks make an excellent path where an old-world look is required. Don't use ordinary bricks — ask for paving ones. As an alternative you can use brick-like blocks (paviors) made of clay or concrete
STONE & SLABS		Natural stone gives an air of luxury, but slate, sandstone, yorkstone etc are very expensive. Slabs made of concrete or reconstituted stone are a much more popular and inexpensive alternative these days
MACADAM		This mixture of stone chippings with tar or bitumen is the favourite material for drives and has several names — asphalt, black top, 'Tarmac' etc. This is not a job for an amateur — choose your contractor with care
CRAZY PAVING		Laying flagstones or paving slabs can be heavy work and you generally have to keep to straight lines — with crazy paving the pieces are smaller and the informal effect means that you don't have to aim for a perfect fit
CONCRETE		Concrete is criticised by many for its austere look, but it remains a popular material for both paths and drives. It is durable, fairly inexpensive and suitable for curving or irregular pathways. Laying concrete is for the fit, strong and knowledgeable
WOOD & BARK		Pulverised or shredded bark has become a popular material for paths in woodland and wild gardens. It is soft underfoot but requires topping up every few years. Sawn log rounds are sometimes set in the shredded bark
GRAVEL & PEBBLES		Gravel is by far the cheapest material. Shingle (small stones smoothed by water) and true gravel (stone chips from a quarry) are the types available. Large rounded pebbles are sometimes used for small decorative areas
PATTERN-PRINTED CONCRETE		A post-war development for paths, drives and patios. A concrete-based mix is poured over the area and a roller is taken over the surface before it is set. The roller leaves an embossed pattern inthe form of blocks, slabs or crazy paving

Lifting & planting perennials

Always check in the A-Z guide of The Flower Expert before lifting a perennial. Some plants hate disturbance. Choose a mild day when the soil is moist. Dig up the clump with a fork. Shake off the excess soil and study where the basic divisions should be. You might be able to break the clump with your hands — if the clump is too tough then use two hand forks or garden forks. Push the forks back-to-back into the centre and prise gently apart. Treat the resulting divisions in a similar fashion or tear apart with the fingers. Select the divisions from the outer region of the clump — remove any weeds.

(4) Plant properly. Fill around the soil ball with loose soil and firm with the fingers or the trowel handle. Water in after planting

(2) Use the right tool. A trowel is generally the best thing to use

(3) Plant at the right depth. Use the old soil mark on the stem as your guide

(1) Dig the hole to fit the roots. The hole should be much wider than it is deep

Taking hardwood cuttings

Hardwood cuttings can be used for many shrubs. Choose a well-ripened shoot of this year's growth.

Best time: November
Examples: Aucuba Cornus Forsythia Ribes Weigela

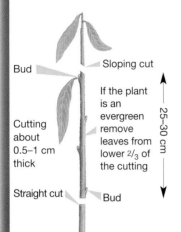

Bud

Sloping cut

Cutting about 0.5–1 cm thick

If the plant is an evergreen remove leaves from lower 2/3 of the cutting

25–30 cm

Straight cut

Bud

4 Leave the top 1/3 of the cutting above ground. Plant the cuttings about 10-15 cm apart. Label the cuttings.

5 Replace the soil a little at a time. Tread down each layer. Fill to ground level – hoe to loosen surface. Water thoroughly.

3 Insert the cutting so that the base rests firmly on the bottom and against the vertical side of the trench.

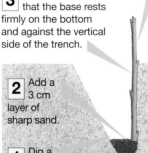

2 Add a 3 cm layer of sharp sand.

1 Dig a 15-20 cm trench with one vertical wall in a well-drained part of the garden. Light shade is desirable.

Firm the soil after winter frosts. Water during dry weather. The cuttings should be ready for planting in about 12 months time.

Filling your window box

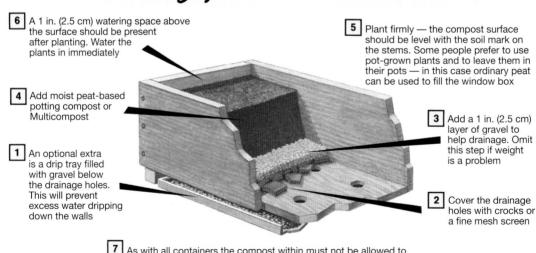

6 A 1 in. (2.5 cm) watering space above the surface should be present after planting. Water the plants in immediately

4 Add moist peat-based potting compost or Multicompost

1 An optional extra is a drip tray filled with gravel below the drainage holes. This will prevent excess water dripping down the walls

5 Plant firmly — the compost surface should be level with the soil mark on the stems. Some people prefer to use pot-grown plants and to leave them in their pots — in this case ordinary peat can be used to fill the window box

3 Add a 1 in. (2.5 cm) layer of gravel to help drainage. Omit this step if weight is a problem

2 Cover the drainage holes with crocks or a fine mesh screen

7 As with all containers the compost within must not be allowed to dry out. Gently fill the watering space above the compost with water if the surface is dry. Watering every day may be necessary if the weather is hot and dry during summer months. Watering upstairs window boxes may be difficult — a number of gadgets including extension lances are available from garden centres

8 Start to feed with a liquid fertilizer 6-8 weeks after planting. Repeat every 1-2 weeks as instructed on the pack. Use a fertilizer with a high potash content

The
first
Expert
1959

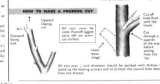

How good is your soil?

ur success as a gardener will depend largely n the condition of your soil. Many people with ... take their soil for granted. They turn it over ... spring, rake it a bit, put in a few seeds or ... and wait for results. They may have to wait ... ng time!

... is a natural mixture of four basic ingre... —SAND, CLAY, CHALK and HUMUS (de... plant and animal remains). Each of these ... ates something to the soil, and when the bal... ween them is just right a loam is formed.

... am is made up of soil crumbs which are ... nutritious footholds for the plant roots. Small ... ces connect these crumbs, carrying air and ... down to the roots. A loam is fertile, free... easy to work with—and rare.

... ur soil is probably nothing like loam. It is ... ore likely to be heavy back-breaking clay, or ... tuff which never seems to get enough water ... at foods. However, there is no need to be too ... arted. Your soil contains all of the ingre... which go to make up a loam, but they are ... in the wrong proportions. With good man... the proper balance can be obtained and ... d turned into an ideal home for plants.

... e of the basic rules of successful gardening is ... ert whatever soil you happen to have into a ... The tables on the following pages will show ... to identify the type of soil you have in your ... and the best way to improve it.

... ake a good long look at your ... l. Good soil sense is the sign ... of the expert gardener.

THE DIFFERENT TYPES OF DRESSINGS

DRESSING — Base dressings are materials added to the soil before or at the time of planting or seed sowing. Their purpose is to provide humus or a steady supply of plant foods during the months to come, therefore HUMUS-MAKERS and SLOW-ACTING FERTILIZERS are generally used.

DRESSING — Once plants are established and growing, the addition of extra plant foods to the soil is known as a top dressing. The usual purpose of a top dressing is to provide quickly-available nourishment to the roots when it is most needed, therefore QUICK-ACTING FERTILIZERS (Liquid plant foods and 'Artificials') are used.

ULCHING — A layer of bulky organic material placed on the soil surface around growing plants is called a mulch. This keeps the soil moist and cool in summer, helps to smother weeds and provides humus and plant foods. Place a mulch around your roses, shrubs and herbaceous border plants in spring or early summer and just see how much hoeing and watering you are spared.

HUMUS-MAKERS, such as rotted animal manure, peat, hop manure, Bio Humus and grass clippings, are used for mulching. Make sure the top-soil is moist before putting the material down, and keep the mulch loose and away from the stems.

YOUR CHOICE OF HUMUS-MAKERS

OIL PESTS

... ts live in the soil. Not all of them, however, are harmful to plants. Some are actually ... ecause they feed on garden pests. A rough guide to follow when digging is—if you can ... ily, kill it.

ANTS steal seeds but do no direct injury to growing plants. However, they loosen the soil around the roots so that plants wilt and die. Ants also carry green-fly from one plant to another, and mulch disfigure the lawn.

WOODLICE are about ⅓ inch long, grey and 'armour-plated'. They hide under decaying refuse, plant pots and so on in the garden and come out at night to attack seedlings and young plants.

SLUGS & SNAILS are serious garden pests, specially when the weather is wet and cool. They hide under stones and debris during the day and come out during the night, devouring seedlings and the roots, stems, leaves and even flowers of mature plants. Slime trails are a clue to their presence.

ODES are sluggish ... grubs which curl up ... d. They do a great ... o seedlings and ... and parts of mature ... ats should not be ... h the helpful centi... brighter coloured ...

LEATHERJACKETS are ... dark grey grubs, about 1 inch ... and very slow-moving. They ... serious nuisance, devouring ... underground parts of a wide range ... plants, including lawn grasses.

EWORMS are one of the most ... n garden pests. They attack the ... ground portion of many plants. ... ms and root crops are holed and the ... stems of chrysanthemums and ... toes hollowed out. Wireworms are ... isk, have about 3 years to live ... re most active in spring ... mmer, and most troublesome in ... -broken grassland.

CHAFER GRUBS are ugly, fat, curved grubs, over 1 inch long. They feed throughout the year on the roots of trees, shrubs, flowers and vegetables which wilt and sometimes die as a result.

CUTWORMS are large, grey or brown caterpillars which attack plants at ground level, so that the leaves wilt and the stems ...

BE YOUR OWN GARDENING EXPERT
BY DR. D. G. HESSAYON

This invaluable book tells you in plain language all you need to know about improving your soil, understanding the needs of your plants, and recognising and dealing with the pests and diseases that attack them. It is full of answers to questions you have so often asked and never been able to find answered in ordinary gardening books.

FREE
SOIL TESTER
INSIDE!

1/6

QUESTIONS		ANSWER	SOIL TYPE	
Choose a day when the soil is moist. Examine the surface and the top two inches. Answer Question 1.				
1	Is the soil very stony—that is, are there scores of large and small stones in a square yard of soil?	YES / NO	STONY / Go on to Question 2	STONY
2	Is the soil dark brown or black, very rich in plant remains, and spongy in texture?	YES / NO	PEATY / Go on to Question 3	PEATY
3	Is the surface soil dark, with white sub-soil a few inches below the surface?	YES / NO	CHALKY / Go on to Question 4	CHALKY
Most people will have answered 'No' to the first three questions. Now pick up a handful of moist soil and mould it with the fingers. Answer Question 4.				
4	Does the soil feel gritty?	YES / NO	Go on to Question 5	
5	When moulded in the hand does it form a ball without crumbling?	YES / NO	LIGHT LOAM / LOAMY SAND	SANDY
6	Does the soil feel sticky?	YES / NO	MEDIUM LOAM / Go on to Question 7	LOAM
Now squeeze a small quantity of the soil with a sliding motion between finger and thumb. Answer Question 7.				
7	Does the surface of the soil become shiny?	YES / NO	Go on to Question 8	
8	Is it hard to change the shape of the soil ball with finger and thumb?	YES / NO	HEAVY LOAM / CLAY	CLAYEY
			CLAY LOAM	

THE GOOD AND BAD POINTS OF YOUR SOIL

TYPE	ADVANTAGES	DISADVANTAGES
NY	Generally free draining Workable early in the season	Dries out very quickly in summer Difficult to cultivate
NG SOIL	Easily worked	

... ose of the soil in your garden ... lants. Whether you make your ... large lawn or a patchwork ... er beds a matter of personal ... ere are basic rules for all ... plants of your choice—and ... this chapter.

ED SOWING

... the easiest and cheapest method ... lants and is the method used for ... ce of mature flowers.

OUTDOORS

... ominate, a seed must have warmth, ... The approximate sowing times ... give you a guide to when the ... ght for germination, but remem... conditions are more important ... hold the operations if the ... d not even, though it may ... range of weeks later.

... to make sure that the seeds have enough air ... d moisture, and that the little roots will have a ... easy foot-hold, a well-made seed-bed is essential. ... make this, choose a day when the soil is ... moist under the surface but quite dry on top. ... lightly tread down the soil and then rake until ... the top is even and crumbly. ... When the seed bed is ready, seeds may be ... roadcast over the surface. But it is more usual

SEEDS SOWN DIRECTLY IN THE BORDER OR VEGETABLE PLOT

The following seeds are sown in the border or vegetable plot, and the seedlings are not transferred to other quarters. As soon as the seedlings reach this stage they are 'thinned out'. This means that they are reduced in number to one seedling to every inch or two. Later on, this thinning is repeated, so that the young plants stand apart at the distance recommended for them.

NAME	WHEN TO SOW	DISTANCE BETWEEN DRILLS	DISTANCE BETWEEN PLANTS AFTER THINNING
ALYSSUM			12 in.
CALANDRINIA			12 in.
CALENDULA			12 in.
CANARY CREEPER			12 in.
CANDYTUFT			9 in.
CHRYSANTHEMUM (ANNUAL)			12 in.
CLARKIA			9 in.
CONVOLVULUS			12 in.
CORNFLOWER		BETWEEN	12 in.
DIMORPHOTHECA		LATE MARCH	9 in.
ESCHSCHOLTZIA		AND THE	9 in.
FLAX		END OF APRIL	12 in.
GODETIA			9 in.
GYPSOPHILA			12 in.
LARKSPUR			12 in.
LAVATERA			18 in.
LOVE-IN-A-MIST			9 in.
MALOPE			12 in.
MIGNONETTE			9 in.
NASTURTIUM			12 in.
NIGHT-SCENTED STOCK			9-12 in.
POPPY			9 in.
STOCK			9 in.
SUNFLOWER			24 in.
SWEET PEA			6 in.
SWEET SULTAN			9 in.
VIRGINIAN STOCK			6 in.
VISCARIA			DO NOT THIN
BEANS, BROAD	MARCH-APRIL		2-3 ft.
BEANS, DWARF FRENCH	MAY-JUNE		1 ft.
BEANS, RUNNER	MAY-JUNE		1 ft.
BEET	APRIL		8 in.
CARROT	MARCH-JULY		3 in.
LETTUCE	MARCH-AUGUST		9 in.
ONION	MARCH-AUGUST		6 in.
PARSLEY	MARCH-AUGUST		3 in.
PEAS	MARCH-JUNE		2-4 ft.
PARSNIP	FEB-MARCH		8 in.
RADISH	MARCH-AUGUST		1 in.
SPINACH	MARCH-AUGUST		6 in.

E WAY TO DIG

Correct digging is an art. The full depth of the blade is called a 'spit'—9 to 10 inches. Drive the spade in vertically with the ball or heel of the foot. Lever the soil up on to the blade by pulling down on the handle, and with a flick of the wrist turn the soil into the trench in front. Turn the spadeful right over to bury weeds completely.

Be methodical. Dig out a trench one foot wide and one foot deep at one end of the plot and cart the soil to the other end of it. Work in strips, turning each one into the trench in front until the plot is dug, and then use the carted soil from the first trench to fill the last one. If the plot is very wide, divide it into sections and deal with them separately.

Dig at the right time. Autumn is the best time, the soil being left as rough as possible for the frost to break down the clods. Sandy soils can be dug during the winter and early spring. Cultivated soil should be left to settle for at least a month before planting.

Use the proper method for the job in hand

Use plain digging on land that has already been cultivated by double digging. Should be carried out annually, except where land is permanently planted.

Dig out trench, and carry soil to back of plot. Spread compost or manure on soil surface. Turn strip A into trench, then combine with B, C etc.

Use double digging on land which has not been cultivated previously. Repeat every 2 years on vegetable plots and every 4 years on flower beds.

Dig out trench, and carry soil to back of plot. Fork over the bottom of the trench to a depth of 1 spit, forking into it compost or manure and 3 oz. bone meal per yard run. Turn strip A into trench. Fork over trench left by removal of A, again incorporating manure and bone meal. Turn over strip B.

Use on stiff clay soils, because ridging exposes the maximum possible area to the action of frost and wind.

Save first three spadefuls for finishing off. Turn centre spadeful forward into trench. Turn B & C on to the side of the trench leaving A on the bottom, so as to form a ridge. Finished Work.

said the spade... to the earthworm

TO DIG OR NOT TO DIG?

In the view of nearly all gardening experts, good digging is the foundation of good gardening.

The value of digging is to break up the soil by direct action and by exposing it to the action of frost and drying winds. This improves drainage, and allows air to get to the lower reaches of the soil. This makes the soil warmer, which means earlier and quicker plant growth in the spring. Also, the natural process of humus decay is speeded up, so that more plant foods are made available.

The division between the digging and the no-digging gardeners is not as wide as many people think. Both sides agree on the value of good compost. The diggers, however, consider the spade to be more efficient than the worm for turning-in and breaking up the soil.

A number of gardeners believe that digging is not necessary, as worms are quite capable of doing the job of the spade.

By the no-digging method, a layer of well-rotted, chopped-up compost is rolled in at the end of October or in the spring. Seeds are sown in the compost.

Further compost dressings are applied each year, to replace the material which has been pulled down by the worms.

... to spade cut is ample.

... lighter colour—due to lack of humus. When digging, it should not be brought to the surface.

... and summer, apply a top dressing of SULPHATE OF AMMONIA as a 'boost' to quick growth.

FEEDING TOMATOES
Correct tomato feeding provides sufficient phosphates and potash to produce stocky plants bearing full trusses of top-quality fruit. The analysis of P.B.I. TOMATO FERTILIZER is 5. 8.1: 10 and is therefore well-suited for this job.

BEFORE PLANTING — Under glass. Fork in 3 oz. per square yard, about 1 week before planting. Water in. Outdoors: Fork in 4 oz. per square yard about 1 week before planting. Water in.

AFTER PLANTING — Do not begin feeding until the first truss has set. Then sprinkle 2 oz. per square yard around the plants every 10-14 days until the final truss has set. Water before and after feeding. For pots, use 1 teaspoonful per plant. Alternatively, BIO PLANT FOOD can be used (see page 14).

FEEDING FRUIT TREES & BUSHES — Let the appearance of the bush or tree be your guide. If the plant is making a lot of leaf but very few flowers, apply a dressing of BONEMEAL and SULPHATE OF POTASH (see page 12). If, on the other hand, the plant is stunted, apply SULPHATE OF AMMONIA instead.

BEDDING PLANTS, CHRYSANTHEMUMS AND DAHLIAS
Fork 2 oz. of FLOWER FERTILIZER per square yard into the bed before planting. When the plants are established, feed with BIO PLANT FOOD (see page 14).

FEEDING ROSES
P.B.I. ROSE FERTILIZER is an organic-based mixture and contains both quick-acting and slow-releasing fertilizers, giving an analysis of 5.2: 9. 6.

BEFORE PLANTING — Fork 4 oz. per square yard into the top soil, 1-2 weeks prior to planting.

AFTER PLANTING — Sprinkle 4 oz. per square yard around the bushes or trees in April. Carefully rake in, and water if the soil is dry.

Apply 2 oz. per square yard around the plants every month throughout the flowering season, beginning when the flower buds first appear. Alternatively, BIO PLANT FOOD can be used (see page 14).

TREE FRUIT

RED SPIDER — Leaves silvery. Fungus outgrowth from stem. Cherry, Apple — SILVER LEAF

Quick-moving, pale green insects. Shoots weak and leaves and trunk — Apple, Pear, Plum — CAPSID

White, powdery deposit — Apple, Pear — MILDEW

Rings of yellowish mould. Fruit rotten — All fruits — BROWN ROT

Leaves raised, shoots distorted — All fruit — GREENFLY

White woolly masses on branches — Apple, Pear — WOOLLY APHID

Dark-coloured patches on leaves and corky areas on fruit — Apple, Pear — SCAB

Sunken rotten area on branches — Apple, Pear — CANKER

Blossoms 'capped' (brown and un-capped growth) — Apple — APPLE BLOSSOM WEEVIL

Tiny yellow insects. Leaves curl and pucker — Apple, Pear — SUCKER

Leaves spun and spun together. Fruit damaged — Apple, Pear, Cherry, Plum — TORTRIX MOTH CATERPILLAR

Earwig-type fruitlets, with grub inside — Apple, Pear — MIDGE

Leaves eaten, green caterpillars present — Apple, Pear, Plum, Cherry — WINTER MOTH CATERPILLAR

MAGGOTY FRUIT

SAWFLY — Chrysanthemus ribbon-like scar. Fat, creamy-white grub inside fruit. Fruit has an objectionable smell when cut open. Attacked fruit generally falls in June or July. Grub may then be seen in soil. — Apple, Plum

CODLING MOTH — Pale pink grub with a brown head. Fruit may not have an objectionable smell when cut open. Grubs can be found in the fruit in July and August. — Apple, Pear, Plum

SOFT FRUIT

GOOSEBERRY SAWFLY / AMERICAN GOOSEBERRY MILDEW — Gooseberry

RASPBERRY CANE SPOT / RASPBERRY MOSAIC / RASPBERRY BEETLE — Raspberry

STRAWBERRY MILDEW / VIRUS — Strawberry

BLACKCURRANT BIG BUD — Blackcurrant

GREY MOULD / SLUGS, SNAILS, BLACK BEETLES / LEAF SPOT — various

PEACH LEAF CURL — Leaves of peaches and almonds distorted, thickened and reddish.

Tree shapes

COLUMNAR (FASTIGIATE) — CONICAL — PYRAMIDAL — ROUND-HEADED — OPEN

WEEPING (PENDULOUS) — PROSTRATE — GLOBULAR (ROUND) — HORIZONTALLY-BRANCHED — LOW-BRANCHED

Restoring an overgrown rockery

Remove all surface rubbish and cut back all overgrown carpeting perennials — dig out all dead plants. Weed control is essential — pull out all annual weeds and self-sown alpines growing in the wrong place. Perennial weeds are a difficult problem when the roots are too deep to be removed — the answer is to paint the leaves very carefully with glyphosate gel. When the weeds are growing within the clump it will be necessary to lift, divide, carefully pull away the weeds and their roots and then replant as described below. Make up a planting mixture of 1 part topsoil, 1 part grit and 1 part peat or well-rotted leaf mould. It is now time for planting. Leave the good specimens, divide up old clumps and buy pots of new specimens. Plan to cover some but not all the rock faces with carpeting plants and aim for year-round colour.

Dig a hole which is clearly larger than the soil ball and fill with water. When it has drained away put in the root ball and fill the space around it with planting mixture. Firm the mixture with your fingers and water in. Cover the surface with grit or stone chippings.

Fences & the law

The basic rule is that you must seek planning permission before building a boundary wall or fence which is more than 2 m high. If the wall or fence is to be erected adjacent to a highway, then you will require planning permission if it is to be more than 1 m high.

Unfortunately, it isn't always quite that simple. For example, seek permission irrespective of height if your house is on a corner site or if the fence you plan to erect could obstruct pedestrians.

In addition check the deeds of your house. These will tell you if walls or fences are banned or restricted — the construction material may be specified. The deeds will also tell you whether the fence line is yours or your neighbours. It is usually easier to tell this on site — the posts and rails nearly always face the owner's property.

A few councils have bye-laws which require householders to maintain their fences, but in nearly all areas there is no law which compels your neighbour to do so. If all else fails, your only answer to a neighbouring faulty fence will be to erect a new one on your side of the boundary line.

Greenhouse tomato types

ORDINARY varieties (O)

This group of red salad Tomatoes contains the traditional-sized fruiting varieties and includes several old favourites which are grown for reliability (Moneymaker), flavour (Ailsa Craig) or earliness (Harbinger).

F_1 HYBRID varieties (F_1)

This group bears fruit which is similar in appearance to the Ordinary versions, but these modern crosses have two important advantages — they are generally heavier yielding and also have a high degree of disease resistance.

BEEFSTEAK varieties (B)

This group produces the large and meaty Tomatoes which are so popular in the U.S and on the Continent. They are excellent for sandwiches but not for frying. There are two types which are grown under glass — the true 'Beefsteak' hybrids such as Dombito and the giant hybrids such as Big Boy. Stop the plants when the fourth truss has set and provide support for the fruit if necessary.

CHERRY varieties (C)

The Cherry- or bite-sized Tomato is much smaller than the fruit from an Ordinary variety, but the flavour is outstanding. The long trusses bear a remarkable number of fruits, but total yield is generally lower than the crop from an Ordinary type of Tomato.

NOVELTY varieties (N)

There are yellow fruits, striped ones and Tomatoes which are Plum-shaped. Some catalogues sing the praises of yellow Tomatoes, but it is hard to tell when they are ripe and they remain unpopular. The first Tomatoes sent to Europe from America were gold-coloured and not red, but that was long ago.

Tree galls

These swellings may occur on all types of plants but are met most frequently on shrubs and trees. They are caused by the plant's reaction to the irritation caused by pests or fungi. In some cases they are large and colourful, and may even be decorative. **Purse gall** and **pouch gall** are caused by aphids, **pineapple gall** on conifers is caused by adelgids, **oak apple** and many other tree galls are due to gall wasps, **lime leaf galls** are due to mites and **azalea gall** is caused by a fungus. In nearly all cases there is little or no harm to the plant. Cut off and burn if unsightly.

Oak apple

Lime leaf gall

Azalea gall

House plant miscellany

The Survey Scene: OUR FAVOURITE PLANTS

AZALEA

BEGONIA

CACTI & SUCCULENTS

CHLOROPHYTUM (Spider plant)

CYCLAMEN

DIEFFENBACHIA (Dumb cane)

FERNS

FICUS (Weeping fig)

GERANIUM

HEDERA (Ivy)

KALANCHOE

MONSTERA (Swiss cheese plant)

ORCHIDS

PALMS

POINSETTIA

POT CHRYSANTHEMUM

SAINTPAULIA (African violet)

SCINDAPSUS

SPATHIPHYLLUM (Peace lily)

SPRING BULBS

Many plants from the 1990 surveys have kept their place — Christmas favourites such as Azalea, Cyclamen and Poinsettia remain and so do the palms, ferns and ivy. But there have been some quite drastic changes. Orchids were not included in the top 20 in the earlier surveys, but they are now number 3 in the list. The rise of the peace lily is even more surprising, moving from outside the top 20 to number 2. The top spot is held by spring bulbs.

Datura suaveolens

In the beginning: PEACE LILY

Spathiphyllum wallisii first came to Europe in 1824. It was found by Gustav Wallis in the swampy Colombian jungle — he sent it to various European botanical gardens but it was never again found in the wild. Wallis is remembered in its latin name, but its common names (peace lily and white sails) only came into use when it was developed as a house plant. This glossy-leaved species grows about 40 cm high — once the only type available, but it lost its crown to the larger-flowered and more fragrant variety Mauna Loa. In recent years it is the smaller types such as Gimini which have become great favourites.

TRY GARDEN PLANTS INDOORS

There are many plants in the outdoor section of the garden centre which can be grown as house plants. Listed below are ones which are readily available.

AGAPANTHUS	FERNS
ASTILBE	FUCHSIA
AUCUBA	GARDEN BULBS
BEDDING PLANTS	GERANIUM
BUXUS	HEBE
CALCEOLARIA	HEDERA
CALLISTEMON	HYDRANGEA
CAMELLIA	LAURUS
CELOSIA	MYRTUS
CHRYSANTHEMUM	NANDINA
COLEUS	PRIMULA
EUONYMUS	VIBURNUM
FATSIA	YUCCA

Name that shrub

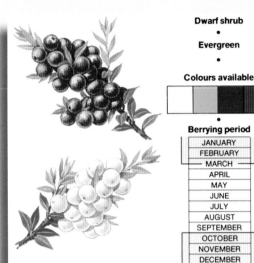

Dwarf shrub
•
Evergreen
•
Colours available

•
Berrying period

| JANUARY |
| FEBRUARY |
| MARCH |
| APRIL |
| MAY |
| JUNE |
| JULY |
| AUGUST |
| SEPTEMBER |
| OCTOBER |
| NOVEMBER |
| DECEMBER |

One of the best of all the berrying bushes. Birds don't like the large, porcelain-like fruits and so they remain on the suckering bush from early autumn until early spring. The bush grows about waist-high and spreads steadily to form a dense thicket. In May or June the creamy-white flowers appear — bell-shaped and pendent. These blooms are either male or female and are nearly always borne on separate plants, so you have to grow a group (one male to three to five female varieties) to make sure that berries will be produced. The dark green leaves are about 1/2 in. long and are stiff and prickly.

Answer on page 128

Orchid miscellany

Viagra — orchid style

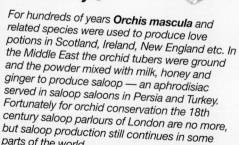

For hundreds of years **Orchis mascula** and related species were used to produce love potions in Scotland, Ireland, New England etc. In the Middle East the orchid tubers were ground and the powder mixed with milk, honey and ginger to produce saloop — an aphrodisiac served in saloop saloons in Persia and Turkey. Fortunately for orchid conservation the 18th century saloop parlours of London are no more, but saloop production still continues in some parts of the world.

Lily types

TURK'S-CAP SHAPED LILIES
The petals are rolled and swept back. The flowers are usually small.

Examples: **L. martagon, L. 'Mrs. R.O. Backhouse', L. hansonii, L. 'Dalhansonii'**

TRUMPET SHAPED LILIES
The petals are grouped together for part of the length of the flower to produce a basal tube.

Examples: **L. regale, L. 'Limelight', L. candidum, L. longiflorum**

BOWL SHAPED LILIES
The petals flare open to produce a wide bowl. The flowers are usually large.

Examples: **L. auratum, L. 'Pink Glory', L. 'Crimson Beauty'**

Arch types

Flat-topped arch	Round-topped arch	Pointed or apex arch	Ogee or gothic arch	Hedge archway	Moon gate

Anatomy of a child-friendly garden

Wild area
Older children want an area where they can play and not be seen from the house. Ideally there should be trees, logs etc for make-believe games

Nature area
A bird table and bird bath give children the chance to study nature close at hand

Paddling pool
An inflatable one is best — empty after use and put away. Great fun on hot days, but never leave a toddler unattended

Low fence
A low fence around the border or beds will give protection against rolling balls and some protection against trampling feet

Cycle track
Some designers advise a path around the garden along which children can ride their bicycles or tricycles

Sand pit
A ground-level sand pit or raised sand box is a great delight for toddlers. Make one (see page 77) or buy one — site it close to the house so you can keep a watchful eye

Lawn
An essential feature for ball- and chasing-games. Place goalposts away from windows

Playground
An equipment area for older children — a strong arch which can hold swing or climbing rope. Other alternatives are slide, see-saw or climbing frame. Base should be soft grass or bark chippings

Children's garden
A very useful feature if the whole garden is not enclosed by a fence. A simple picket fence with a gate keeps children from wandering away and provides an area which they can feel belongs to them. Provide a soft base (grass or bark chippings) and include items such as a playhouse, miniature furniture, flower bed for seeds, etc

Rogues gallery

ROSE MILDEW

This form of powdery mildew is the most widespread rose disease. A white, powdery mould develops on leaves, buds and shoots. Affected leaves curl and may fall prematurely — diseased buds may not open properly. The disease is encouraged by closed-in conditions, dryness at the roots, poor feeding and by hot days which are followed by cold nights. Climbers growing against walls are especially susceptible — ensure there is adequate air space between the wires and the bricks. Some roses are much more resistant than others — check before buying. Cut off and burn badly infected shoots when pruning, use a balanced and not a nitrogen-rich fertilizer when feeding and mulch in spring. Spray with myclobutanil or penconazole when the first spots are seen — repeat every 2 weeks. If mildew is a recurrent problem in your garden, begin spraying as leaf buds open.

Why plants fail to flower properly

• Impatience
A recently-planted perennial may not bloom in the first season after planting. Some border plants such as peonies hate being moved.

• Too much shade
Some perennials demand a sunny site. Always check the light requirements of any plant you propose to buy.

• Pests and diseases
A number of insects and fungal diseases can kill or distort flowers — see The Flower Expert for identification.

• Old age
Plants can deteriorate with age. The answer is to lift and divide.

• Too little water
Drought results in a sub-standard display if you fail to water. Apply a mulch in late spring. Water in dry weather before the leaves start to suffer.

• Late frost
A late frost can kill the buds on plants which are not fully hardy. Avoid plants which are known to be slightly tender if you live in a hard-winter area. You can protect a semi-hardy plant when frost is forecast by draping horticultural fleece over the stems.

• Poor feeding
The plants may be hungry. The feed to use is one with a potash (K) content higher than the nitrogen (N) one — the pack will have this information.

Anatomy of a greenhouse

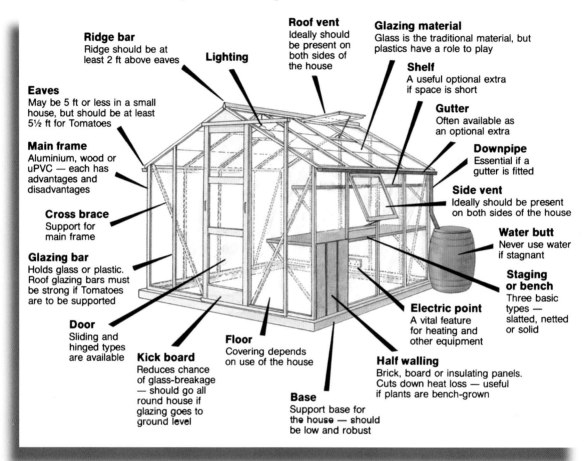

Ridge bar
Ridge should be at
least 2 ft above eaves

Lighting

Roof vent
Ideally should
be present on
both sides of
the house

Glazing material
Glass is the traditional material, but
plastics have a role to play

Shelf
A useful optional extra
if space is short

Gutter
Often available as
an optional extra

Downpipe
Essential if a
gutter is fitted

Side vent
Ideally should be present
on both sides of the house

Water butt
Never use water
if stagnant

**Staging
or bench**
Three basic
types —
slatted, netted
or solid

Eaves
May be 5 ft or less in a small
house, but should be at least
5½ ft for Tomatoes

Main frame
Aluminium, wood or
uPVC — each has
advantages and
disadvantages

Cross brace
Support for
main frame

Glazing bar
Holds glass or plastic.
Roof glazing bars must
be strong if Tomatoes
are to be supported

Door
Sliding and
hinged types
are available

Kick board
Reduces chance
of glass-breakage
— should go all
round house if
glazing goes to
ground level

Floor
Covering depends
on use of the house

Base
Support base for
the house — should
be low and robust

Electric point
A vital feature
for heating and
other equipment

Half walling
Brick, board or insulating panels.
Cuts down heat loss — useful
if plants are bench-grown

Conservatory window types

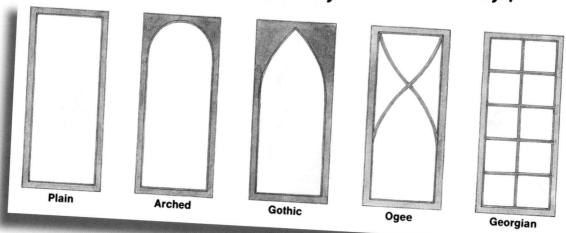

Plain

Arched

Gothic

Ogee

Georgian

Strawberry types

SUMMER FRUITING STRAWBERRY
(Other names: **Single Crop, June Bearer**)

By far the most popular group. Largest and best quaity fruits found here. Cropping time between late May and late July. Single flush — a few varieties occasionally produce a second crop.
Productive life: 3-4 years

ALPINE STRAWBERRY
(Other name: **Wild**)

Fruit is very small — aromatic ans sweet but not juicy.
Grow in a container or as an edging.
Sow seed in autumn — plant out in spring. Cropping time midsummer to late autumn. Red, yellow and white varieties are available.
Productive life: 1 year

PERPETUAL STRAWBERRY
(Other names: **Remontant, Everbearer, Autumn Fruiting, Two Crop**)

Fruit is generally smaller and less sweet than summer fruiting varieties — plants are less hardy. Cropping time June and again in late summer-autumn. Remove early flowers to increase the autumn crop.
Productive life: 2 years

DAY NEUTRAL STRAWBERRY

Only a few varieties available. Outdoors they behave like ordinary perpetuals in Britain — under glass they will produce winter fruit 12 weeks after planting. Remove early flowers in the garden to increase the autumn crop.
Productive life: 2 years

Skeletonising leaves

Skeletonised leaves are available from some larger florists and garden centres, providing unusual material to serve as an attractive background feature in floral arrangements. Unfortunately it is not easy to find a supplier and the range of shapes is limited. Obviously a do-it-yourself technique would be useful, but most experts regard skeletonising as a job for the professionals. However, with patience and a little luck you can produce these leaves at home.

You may be lucky enough to find naturally-skeletonised leaves half-buried in the debris beneath the branches of Camellia, Holly or Rhododendron, but it is usually necessary to start from scratch. Choose large leaves — Oak, Camellia, Laurel, Maple, Rhododendron and Magnolia are suitable subjects. The leaves should be free from blemishes — they should be mature and healthy. Stir a handful of washing soda in a large enamel saucepan half-filled with soft water and boil the leaves for about an hour. Put on rubber or plastic gloves and remove one leaf to see if you can rub off some of the soft green tissue under a running tap. If the soft tissue is still firmly attached, continue the boiling process for another hour.

Remove the leaves one at a time. Lay each one in turn on a piece of absorbent paper and scrape off all the soft tissue with the back of a knife. Rinse under a running tap and repeat the process until a clean leaf skeleton is obtained. Do not remove the next leaf from the soda solution until you have properly skeletonised the first one. Soak each skeletonised leaf in dilute bleach and then spread them on absorbant paper to dry. For curled leaves wrap around a pencil or candle. After a day or two they will be ready. The leaf stem will be weak and will have to be wired for support. Now you have your own home-made skeletonised leaves.

Common lawn weeds

BELLIS PERENNIS
(Daisy)

A major weed, especially in closely-mown turf. Occasional plants may not be a problem, but the creeping stems can produce extensive mats if neglected. Grub out clumps or use a selective weedkiller. A repeat treatment after 6 weeks may be needed.

PLANTAGO MAJOR
(Greater plantain)

The most serious of the plantain weeds — can be a major nuisance in compacted soil areas. Leaves are broadly oval with long stalks. Hand weed isolated specimens — spot-treat or spray large clumps with a selective weedkiller in spring.

RANUNCULUS REPENS
(Creeping buttercup)

The most serious of the buttercup weeds. Runners creep along the surface and root at intervals — the stalks bear typical buttercup flowers in May-August. Dig out isolated clumps — larger areas can be controlled by using a selective weedkiller.

SAGINA PROCUMBENS
(Pearlwort)

A major weed, especially in closely-mown turf. The creeping stems spread from the small rosettes to form a dense mat. Use a selective weedkiller when the grass is actively growing — a single treatment is generally sufficient. Feed in spring.

TARAXACUM
OFFICINALE
(Dandelion)

A major weed in all types of soil. Large leaves with ragged edges form flat rosettes. Hand weeding is practical, but remaining root bits produce new plants. Spot-treat with a selective weedkiller — repeat 6 weeks later.

TRIFOLIUM REPENS
(White clover)

A major weed which occurs everywhere. Runners creep along the surface and root at intervals. White or pinkish flower-heads. Rake before mowing. Water in dry weather. Use a selective weedkiller in June or July — one treatment should be sufficient.

Hyacinth types

DUTCH HYACINTHS

H. orientalis 'Pink Pearl'

MULTIFLORA HYACINTHS

H. orientalis 'Multiflora'

ROMAN HYACINTHS

H. orientalis albulus

Treating wood

Most softwoods are susceptible to rot when used outdoors, and so it is essential to use some form of protective treatment prior to exposure to the elements. Some people choose white paint for fences and gates, but the usual choice is a preservative which contains a stain. Whichever material you choose, read the section below before you begin the treatment.

PRESERVATIVES

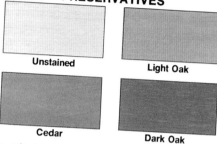

Unstained · Light Oak · Cedar · Dark Oak

The rule is worth repeating — make sure that softwood items for the garden have been pressure-treated before you buy them. If they have not or if you have made your own then you will have to apply a suitable product. Most products are oil- or solvent-based and should be kept away from naked flames — wear gloves when applying such preservatives and keep well away from foliage. The water-based products are harmless to plants, but may be less effective. Brushing-on is the usual application method, and is satisfactory for top-up treatment, but for fresh wood the immersion method is much better. Stand posts in a bucket or place boards in a shallow bath containing preservative for at least an hour. This is essential if the wood will be in contact with the ground. Colourless preservatives are available, but the usual choice is a product which contains an oak or cedar stain.

Mammal tracks

Most mammals feed at night so you might not see them, but you will find their tracks in snow or mud. These impressions are not to scale.

Hedgehog · Wood mouse · Dog · Muntjac · Squirrel · Rabbit · Cat · Fox · Badger

Buying cut flowers

WHERE TO BUY

A long-established florist obviously has a reputation to maintain, but you cannot rely on one supplier always being superior to the others. The only way to judge quality is to look at the stock — go somewhere else if the water in the flower buckets is stale and if full-price material is well past the stage described below. Most keen flower arrangers establish a relationship with a local supplier so that orders can be placed for out-of-the-ordinary flowers which are not kept in stock but are available at the wholesale market.

WHAT TO LOOK FOR

Look at the flower buckets first. They should be out of direct sunlight and the water should be clear and not smelly. The foliage should be firm and the cut ends properly immersed. As a general rule choose blooms at the **Open Stage** for a long-lasting display. At this stage multi-flowered stems have a few open blooms and plenty of coloured buds. The **Bud Stage** is too early — tight green buds do not often open indoors. The problem with the **Ripe Stage** is that all the flowers are fully open and so the display will be short-lived. Of course this is not a problem if the display is for a special occasion on the next day. With single Daisy-like blooms the Open Stage is when the petals are fully open but the central disc is free from a dusting of yellow pollen. These are general rules — see below for specific guidance.

WHEN TO BUY THE POPULAR ONES

PLANT	STAGE OF DEVELOPMENT FOR MAXIMUM VASE-LIFE
ALSTROEMERIA	A few flowers open — buds showing colour
ANEMONE	Most flowers open — centres still tight. Buds showing colour
CARNATION — SPRAY	About half flowers open — buds plump and firm
CARNATION — STANDARD	Flowers open — no white threads. Leaves firm and fresh
CHRYSANTHEMUM — SINGLE	Most flowers open. Central discs greenish — no pollen present
CHRYSANTHEMUM — DOUBLE	Flowers open — centres tight and outer petals firm
DAFFODIL — SINGLE	Buds showing colour and beginning to open
DAFFODIL — DOUBLE	Flowers fully open
FREESIA	A few flowers open — buds showing colour
GERBERA	Flowers open. Central disc greenish — no pollen present
GLADIOLUS	A few flowers open — buds showing colour
GYPSOPHILA	Nearly all flowers open
IRIS	A few flowers open — buds showing colour
LILY	A few flowers open — buds showing colour
ORCHID	Flowers fully open
RANUNCULUS	Most flowers open — centres still tight. Buds showing colour
ROSE	Open buds or tight-centred flowers. Some leaves on stems
STATICE	Nearly all flowers open
TULIP	Buds showing colour — leaves not limp

Bricklaying technique

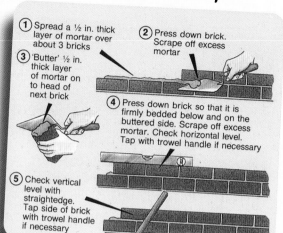

① Spread a ½ in. thick layer of mortar over about 3 bricks

② Press down brick. Scrape off excess mortar

③ 'Butter' ½ in. thick layer of mortar on to head of next brick

④ Press down brick so that it is firmly bedded below and on the buttered side. Scrape off excess mortar. Check horizontal level. Tap with trowel handle if necessary

⑤ Check vertical level with straightedge. Tap side of brick with trowel handle if necessary

Orchid miscellany

The Ghost Orchid

Dendrophyllax lindenii in full flower is a sight to remember, but unfortunately you are unlikely to see this rarity in its native home. Its matted roots cling to trees growing in the swamps of Florida and Cuba, and the odd feature is that there are no leaves — it is the job of the roots to take in water and minerals, manufacture carbohydrates and produce the nutrients the plant needs.

In summer the sweet-smelling flowers appear, and these blooms appear to float in the air — hence the common name. The lip bears leg-like tails and the reason for the alternative name of Frog Orchid is obvious.

Building a sand pit

STEP 5:
MAKE THE EDGE
Place a row of 1½ ft x 1½ ft paving slabs all round the edge after refilling the gap between the boards and the soil. Bed down the slabs in blobs of mortar

STEP 4:
FILL WITH SAND
Add a 9 in. layer of silver sand — do not use sharp nor building sand

STEP 3:
FIX THE BOTTOM
Place a piece of hardboard at the bottom — it need not fit exactly. Drill a few ½ in. holes for drainage

DIY Sand box

DIY Sand box in kit form

STEP 2:
FIX THE SIDES
Cut 4 planks — 5 ft x 1 ft x 1 in. Use them to line the hole — attach to 1½ ft x 2 in. x 2 in. pointed stakes driven into the ground as shown

STEP 6:
COVER WHEN NOT IN USE
You must cover the pit after play in order to keep out rain, cats and dogs

STEP 1:
DIG THE HOLE
The hole should be about 5½ ft x 5½ ft and 14 in. deep. Spread a 2 in. layer of sand on the surface

Ready-made Plastic sand box with cover

Garden lighting

FLOODLIGHTING

UPLIGHTING

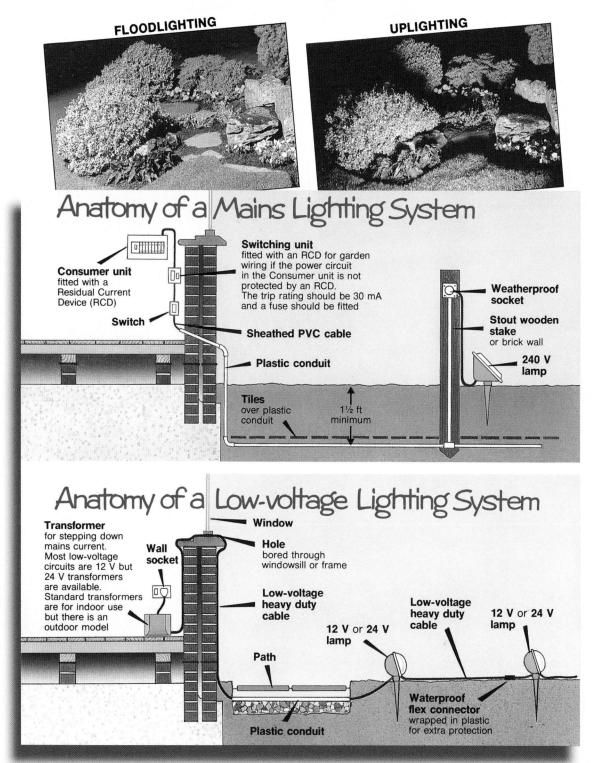

Anatomy of a Mains Lighting System

Consumer unit
fitted with a
Residual Current
Device (RCD)

Switch

Switching unit
fitted with an RCD for garden
wiring if the power circuit
in the Consumer unit is not
protected by an RCD.
The trip rating should be 30 mA
and a fuse should be fitted

Sheathed PVC cable

Plastic conduit

Tiles
over plastic
conduit

$1\frac{1}{2}$ ft
minimum

**Weatherproof
socket**

**Stout wooden
stake**
or brick wall

**240 V
lamp**

Anatomy of a Low-voltage Lighting System

Transformer
for stepping down
mains current.
Most low-voltage
circuits are 12 V but
24 V transformers
are available.
Standard transformers
are for indoor use
but there is an
outdoor model

**Wall
socket**

Window

Hole
bored through
windowsill or frame

**Low-voltage
heavy duty
cable**

Path

Plastic conduit

**12 V or 24 V
lamp**

**Low-voltage
heavy duty
cable**

**12 V or 24 V
lamp**

**Waterproof
flex connector**
wrapped in plastic
for extra protection

Erecting a chain link fence

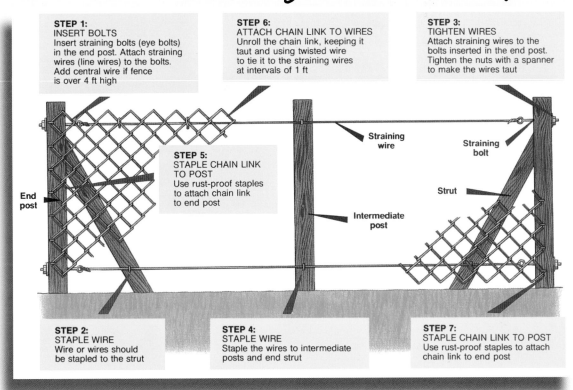

STEP 1:
INSERT BOLTS
Insert straining bolts (eye bolts) in the end post. Attach straining wires (line wires) to the bolts. Add central wire if fence is over 4 ft high

STEP 6:
ATTACH CHAIN LINK TO WIRES
Unroll the chain link, keeping it taut and using twisted wire to tie it to the straining wires at intervals of 1 ft

STEP 3:
TIGHTEN WIRES
Attach straining wires to the bolts inserted in the end post. Tighten the nuts with a spanner to make the wires taut

STEP 5:
STAPLE CHAIN LINK TO POST
Use rust-proof staples to attach chain link to end post

Straining wire

Straining bolt

Strut

End post

Intermediate post

STEP 2:
STAPLE WIRE
Wire or wires should be stapled to the strut

STEP 4:
STAPLE WIRE
Staple the wires to intermediate posts and end strut

STEP 7:
STAPLE CHAIN LINK TO POST
Use rust-proof staples to attach chain link to end post

Anatomy of a flexible liner pond

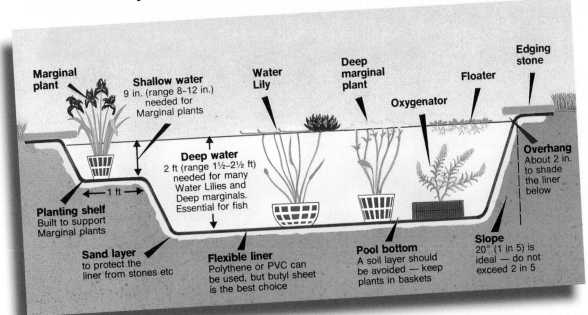

Marginal plant

Shallow water
9 in. (range 8–12 in.) needed for Marginal plants

Water Lily

Deep marginal plant

Oxygenator

Floater

Edging stone

Deep water
2 ft (range 1½–2½ ft) needed for many Water Lilies and Deep marginals. Essential for fish

1 ft

Overhang
About 2 in. to shade the liner below

Planting shelf
Built to support Marginal plants

Sand layer
to protect the liner from stones etc

Flexible liner
Polythene or PVC can be used, but butyl sheet is the best choice

Pool bottom
A soil layer should be avoided — keep plants in baskets

Slope
20° (1 in 5) is ideal — do not exceed 2 in 5

Dealing with a leaking pond

Repairing a concrete pond

The problem may be due to a porous surface because of the use of too much or the wrong type of sand or the presence of a large number of tiny cracks. The answer is to thoroughly clean the surface and then apply two coats of pond sealant. This repair should last for several years.

The other possibility is a distinct crack which is at least 1 cm wide. Undercut the crack with a cold chisel — the prepared crack should be wider below the surface. Remove all dust and fill with a waterproof mastic cement. Finally paint the area with a proprietary sealant. Large cracks are difficult to seal — it is usually better to fill with mortar and then fit a butyl liner.

Repairing a rigid liner pond

Vacuum-formed polyethylene ponds tend to crack after a few years because of the effect of sunlight. You can buy rigid liners guaranteed for 20 years, but even here cracks can appear if the edges are not firmly supported. Cracks are not always easy to locate — try tapping the surface and listening for a different note. Repair kits are available.

Repairing a flexible liner

Locating the crack or hole is not always easy. Press the surface after emptying — an unusually soft spot generally indicates a hole or tear in the liner. Flexible liners have a limited life span, varying from just a few years for cheap polyethylene to 50 years for top quality butyl sheeting.

It is not worth trying to repair a cracked polyethylene-lined pond — remove it and replace with PVC or butyl sheeting. If one of these better quality materials becomes torn or cracked you can buy a repair kit to seal the damaged area. Cut a piece of repair sheet which is twice as long and wide as the tear. Clean the patch and the pond sheeting and apply adhesive. Carefully follow the instructions on the kit package.

Rogues gallery

FIREBLIGHT

A devastating disease of shrubs and trees of the rose family. The tell-tale sign is the presence of brown, wilted leaves which do not fall. Cankers develop on the bark and diseased shoots die back — cut out affected branches to 60 cm below the brown leaves. Trees die when the trunk is infected — remove and burn.

Plant types

ROSES

Deciduous Shrubs and Trees of the genus Rosa, usually listed separately in the catalogues because of their importance and great popularity

A **Half Standard** is a Rose Tree with a 2½ ft stem

A **Full Standard** is a Rose Tree with a 3½ ft stem

EVERGREEN SHRUBS & TREES

Woody plants which retain their leaves during winter

Conifers bear cones and nearly all are Evergreens

Semi-evergreens (e.g Privet) retain most of their leaves in a mild winter

WOODY PLANTS

Perennial plants with woody stems which survive the winter

A **Shrub** bears several woody stems at ground level

A **Tree** bears only one woody stem at ground level

A **Climber** has the ability when established to attach itself to or twine around an upright structure. Some weak-stemmed plants which require tying to stakes (e.g Climbing Roses) are included here

A **Hedge** is a continuous line of Shrubs or Trees in which the individuality of each plant is partly or wholly lost

DECIDUOUS SHRUBS & TREES

Woody plants which shed their leaves in winter

Top Fruit are Trees which produce edible fruit (e.g Apple, Pear, Peach, Plum)

Soft Fruit are Shrubs and Climbers which produce edible fruit (e.g Blackcurrant, Gooseberry). A few are Herbaceous Plants (e.g Strawberry)

A **Ground Cover** is a low-growing and spreading plant which forms a dense, leafy mat

TURF PLANTS

Low-growing carpeting plants, nearly always members of the Grass Family, which can be regularly sheared and walked upon

VEGETABLES

Plants which are grown for their edible roots, stems or leaves. A few are grown for their fruits (e.g Tomato, Cucumber, Marrow, Capsicum)

HERBS

Plants which are grown for their medicinal value, their culinary value as garnishes or flavourings, or their cosmetic value as sweet-smelling flowers or leaves

HERBACEOUS PLANTS

Plants with non-woody stems which generally die down in winter

BULBS

Bulbs (more correctly Bulbous Plants) produce underground fleshy organs which are offered for sale for planting indoors or outdoors. Included here are the **True Bulbs, Corms, Rhizomes** and **Tubers**

BIENNIALS

Plants which complete their life span, from seed to death, in two seasons

A **Hardy Biennial** (HB) is sown outdoors in summer, producing stems and leaves in the first season and flowering in the next

Some Perennials are treated as Biennials (e.g Wallflower, Daisy)

PERENNIALS

Plants which complete their life span, from seed to death, in three or more seasons

A **Hardy Perennial** (HP) will live for years in the garden — the basic plant of the herbaceous border

A **Half-hardy Perennial** (HHP) is not fully hardy and needs to spend its winter in a frost-free place (e.g Fuchsia, Geranium)

A **Greenhouse Perennial** (GP) is not suitable for outdoor cultivation

A **Rockery Perennial** (RP) is a dwarf Hardy Perennial suitable for growing in a rockery. **Alpine** is an alternative name, although some originated on the shore rather than on mountains, and some delicate True Alpines need to be grown indoors

ANNUALS

Plants which complete their life span, from seed to death, in a single season

A **Hardy Annual** (HA) is sown outdoors in spring

A **Half-hardy Annual** (HHA) cannot withstand frost, and so they are raised under glass and planted outdoors when the danger of frost is past

A **Greenhouse** (or **Tender**) **Annual** (GA) is too susceptible to cold weather for outdoor cultivation, but may be planted out for a short time in summer

A **Bedding Plant** is an Annual or Biennial set out in quantity in autumn or spring to provide a temporary display

Dealing with efflorescence

A white deposit frequently appears on the surface of new brickwork. This is due to the water-soluble salts within the bricks being drawn to the outside as the walling materials dry out. Once at the outer face of the brickwork these salts crystalise and appear as a white fluffy film.

This efflorescence is quite normal and all you have to do is to remove the deposit with a wire brush until it ceases to appear. Never try to scrub it away with water — you will only make matters worse by bringing fresh salts to the surface. This efflorescence should not persist for more than a year or two on a free-standing wall, but it can go on for much longer on an earth-retaining one.

The sink garden

A sink garden is made from an old stone or glazed sink in which the drainage hole has been covered with crocks or rubble and then filled with a free-draining compost to 2 in. (5 cm) below the rim. The outer surface can be covered with a cement/sand/peat mixture to give a more natural appearance. Use the sink garden for miniature rockery perennials, dwarf conifers and miniature bulbs. Place some small rocks between the plants and cover the surface with stone chippings.

The mixed border

The mixed border has taken over from the herbaceous border as the most popular way of growing border perennials. Gone are most of the slavish rules about colour, height etc, and the flowering season has been extended by including other types of plants. Like all borders it is designed to be viewed from two or three sides and not from all angles. The shape is often irregular and no longer strictly rectangular. The usual pattern is a framework of flowering shrubs, roses and decorative evergreens. Border perennials form large and colourful patches and close to the front a number of pockets are left to be filled with bulbs and bedding plants.

Name that flower

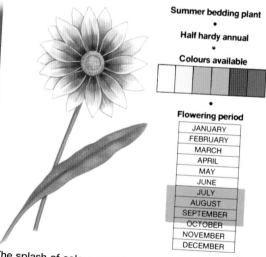

Summer bedding plant
•
Half hardy annual
•
Colours available

Flowering period

| JANUARY |
| FEBRUARY |
| MARCH |
| APRIL |
| MAY |
| JUNE |
| JULY |
| AUGUST |
| SEPTEMBER |
| OCTOBER |
| NOVEMBER |
| DECEMBER |

The splash of colour on a sunny summer day is almost unrivalled in the world of annuals. Each large Daisy-like flower bears petals which arch backwards to reveal the central dark-coloured ring around the disc. The wide range of flower colours comes in all sorts of combinations — blends, stripes, contrasting zones etc. This is a plant for the edge of a sunny bed or rockery. It tolerates drought, salt-laden air and wind but it dislikes heavy soil and the flowers close up in dull weather and in the evening.

Answer on page 128

Gate types

GARDEN GATES

A **garden gate** is a single gate in the boundary wall, fence or hedge. The maximum width for standard pedestrian gates should be 4 ft.

A **side gate** is a 6 ft high door of metal or wood designed to provide security.

Ledged-and-braced gate	Wrought iron gate	Side gate

DRIVE GATES

A **drive gate** closes the driveway used for a car. The usual style is a pair of wooden or metal gates which lock at the centre. Alternatively, a single wide gate such as a five-barred gate may be used. Drive gates should always open inwards.

Double gates	Five-barred gate	Yeoman gate

Taking stem cuttings

Stem-tip cutting

Cut off leaves from lower half of cutting

Leaf joint

Straight cut

Dip bottom ¹/₂ in. (1 cm) into a rooting hormone

Basal cutting

Straight cut or pulled off with heel of old stem attached

Dip bottom ¹/₂ in. (1 cm) into a rooting hormone

Filling up the pot

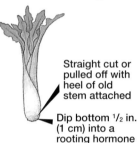

② Trim foliage of large-leaved plants by half

③ Make a hole close to the edge with a pencil

⑤ Water in very gently

① Fill a 5 in. (12.5 cm) pot with a suitable compost

④ Insert cutting — firm around the base with a pencil. Label if necessary

Polythene bag method

① Place four canes in the pot and drape a polythene bag over them. Secure with a rubber band. Stand pot in a bright spot, away from direct sunlight

② Leave undisturbed until new growth appears. Harden off by giving more ventilation and then lift out each rooted cutting after watering — transfer into a compost-filled 3 in. (7.5 cm) pot

Propagator method

① Place pots in the propagator. Keep at 65°-75°F (18°-24°C). Shade and ventilate on hot days

② Leave undisturbed until new growth appears. Harden off by giving more ventilation and then lift out each rooted cutting after watering — transfer into a compost-filled 3 in. (7.5 cm) pot

Cold frame method

① Place pots in a cold frame — shade glass and ventilate on hot days. Water gently when necessary. In frosty weather cover glass with sacking

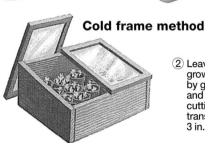

② Leave undisturbed until new growth appears. Harden off by giving more ventilation and then lift out each rooted cutting after watering — transfer into a compost-filled 3 in. (7.5 cm) pot

Easy-care hedging plants

NAME	TYPE	NOTES
ACER (Maple)	F : D	The Field Maple (A. campestre) hedge is much less common than Beech, but it flourishes in all soil types and the plants quickly grow together. Trim in late autumn
BERBERIS (Barberry)	I : D or E	Several evergreens such as B. stenophylla, B. darwinii and B. julianae make splendid informal hedges with yellow flowers in spring. B. thunbergii is deciduous. Trim Berberis after flowering
BERBERIS (Barberry)	D : D	B. thunbergii atropurpurea 'Nana' produces a compact formal hedge about 1½ ft (45 cm) high. The foliage is reddish — trim after leaf fall
CARPINUS (Hornbeam)	F : D	A quick-growing hedge which quickly reaches 8 ft (2.4 m) if left untrimmed. Usually keeps its dead leaves like Beech. Reliable in heavy soil. Trim in late summer
ESCALLONIA (Escallonia)	I : E	The evergreen E. macrantha is popular in coastal areas as it tolerates salt-laden air. Red flowers appear in June — trim when the flowers fade
FAGUS (Beech)	F : D	F. sylvatica has green- and purple-leaved varieties — all can be trimmed to produce a tall formal hedge. Brown leaves persist over winter. Trim in August — tackle any hard pruning in February
ILEX (Holly)	F : E	I. aquifolium forms a dense barrier which is colourful when berries are present or a variegated variety has been used. Trim in late summer
LAVANDULA (Lavender)	D : E	A popular low-growing hedge — purple flowers, aromatic grey foliage. Cut off stalks once flowers fade — trim the plants to shape in April
PRUNUS (Laurel)	F : E	Portugal Laurel (P. lusitanica) and Cherry Laurel (P. laurocerasus) make fine tall hedges with dense shiny leaves, but plenty of room is required. Trim in March
PRUNUS (Sloe)	I : D	The Sloe or Blackthorn (P. spinosa) has long been used for hedging fields —white flowers appear in spring. Cut back unwanted growth in winter
PYRACANTHA (Firethorn)	I : E	The popular P. coccinea can be used for hedging but P. rogersiana is usually recommended. Cut back in summer to expose berries
RIBES (Flowering Currant)	I : D	This plant is usually grown as a shrub, but it can be grown at 1 ft (30 cm) intervals to produce an attractive hedge. Trim when the flowers fade
ROSA (Rose)	I : D	Some Shrub Roses make good hedges, but only informal ones as they cannot stand regular trimming. Remove unwanted growth in spring
TAXUS (Yew)	F : E	This old favourite need not be dull — there are bright golden varieties. No trouble, but it is slow to establish. Trim in late summer
THUJA (Thuja)	F : E	Western Red Cedar (T. plicata) is the conifer to grow if you want cypress-like foliage. Unlike the popular Leyland Cypress it needs only one trim (March) each year

TYPE KEY

F : — Formal Hedge — a line of hedging plants which are trimmed to form a smooth surface. Foliage types are generally treated this way

I : — Informal Hedge — a line of hedging plants which are not trimmed to form a smooth surface. Flowering types are generally treated this way

D : — Dwarf Hedge — a line of low-growing hedging plants which are pruned to 3 ft (90 cm) or less. The hedge may be formal or informal

— : D Deciduous

— : E Evergreen

A Word of Warning

Avoid many of the popular types such as Privet, Lawson's Cypress, Leyland Cypress, Box etc. These hedging plants are not easy-care varieties as they have to be trimmed at least 3 times during the summer months. An easy-care hedging plant is one which requires just one trim a year. A few other hedging plants, such as Honeysuckle, have been omitted from the list because they have an untidy growth habit.

Name that shrub

Dwarf or small shrub

•

Evergreen

•

Colours available

Flowering period

JANUARY
FEBRUARY
MARCH
APRIL
MAY
JUNE
JULY
AUGUST
SEPTEMBER
OCTOBER
NOVEMBER
DECEMBER

This evergreen shrub is of little interest during the spring and summer months — it is low-growing and the lance-shaped or oval leaves are nothing special. But in late winter or early spring it becomes a plant much loved by flower arrangers. Clusters of white- or cream-petalled male flowers and insignificant female flowers are borne all along the stems — a key feature is the very strong fragrance. The blooms are followed by berries — black or red depending on the species.

Answer on page 128

Name that flower

Summer bedding plant

•

Half hardy annual

•

Colours available

•

Flowering period

JANUARY
FEBRUARY
MARCH
APRIL
MAY
JUNE
JULY
AUGUST
SEPTEMBER
OCTOBER
NOVEMBER
DECEMBER

A ground-hugging wide-spreading succulent which provides a summer-long colourful display if the conditions are right. The reddish stems bear clusters of long fleshy leaves which in a sunny season can be almost covered by the saucer-shaped flowers. These blooms are often ruffled and the petals have a distinctive silky sheen. This is one to plant at the front of a sunny bed or in an unshaded rockery — there should be no shade even for a short period during the day.

Answer on page 128

Buying bulbs

Good Signs

Stem growth absent, although a short and thick shoot tip may be acceptable

Neck firm

Surface clean and firm

Bulb heavy for its size

Tunic entire, although cracks or gaps in Tulip skin are acceptable

Base firm (test with finger) and free from rot

Root growth not apparent

Bad Signs

Stem growth clearly present — long, spindly and white or pale green

Neck soft or diseased

Surface dirty and soft

Bulb light for its size

Tunic missing. Tissue below diseased, mouldy, damaged or shrivelled

Base soft — mould present

Root growth clearly active

House plant miscellany

In the beginning: AFRICAN VIOLET

The african violet was a late starter. It is one of the world's favourite house plants, but it was unknown until it was discovered in 1892 by Baron Walter von Saint Paul. He found the small purple-flowered plant in German East Africa (now Tanzania) where he was a regional governor, and sent seeds to his father in Germany. The plant was named Saintpaulia in honour of its discoverer, and within a year specimens were being offered for sale in Germany. At the start of the 20th century it was to be found in a number of European countries, but it was not until 1926 that seeds were imported into the U.S. This was the start of the african violet craze — by 1950 there were over 500 varieties in a wide range of shapes, sizes and colours.

The Survey Scene: HOW MANY PLANTS WE BUY

PLANTS BOUGHT EACH YEAR	%
0	2
1 – 4	66
5 – 10	24
more than 10	6

Nearly one in three households buys at least 5 plants every year.

A simple test for HUMIDITY LEVEL

The atmosphere in a centrally-heated home in midwinter can be as dry as desert air, so it is often useful to know the relative humidity of the rooms where your plants live. You can buy a hygrometer, but the simple guide below will provide you with a quick answer.

Place a tumbler in the refrigerator (not the freezer) overnight. Take it out in the morning and put on a surface away from a radiator or source of steam. Look at the surface after 5 minutes.

Surface frosty at first but it is now clear
The air is dry — most plants will need a moister atmosphere — consider misting, plant grouping, a pebble tray etc.

Surface is frosted
The air is reasonably moist. This is the average situation and most plants should be reasonably happy, although some may need misting.

Surface is frosted — one or more narrow water rivulets have run down the surface
The air is very moist. Nearly all plants should find the air sufficiently moist.

Rogues gallery

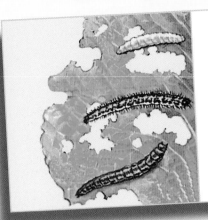

CABBAGE CATERPILLAR

Ragged holes appear in the leaves of brassicas such as cabbage, cauliflower and broccoli. The 2.5 cm **small cabbage white** is velvety — the 4 cm **large cabbage white** is slightly hairy and the **cabbage moth** is smooth. Attacks are worst in hot, dry weather. Pick off if practical or spray with deltamethrin if there is a serious infestation.

Dividing plants

BORDER and ROCKERY PERENNIALS

Division is a form of propagation which is often forced upon you — spreading border perennials will often deteriorate after a few years if not lifted and divided.

Choose a mild day in spring or autumn when the soil is moist. Dig up the clump with a fork, taking care not to damage the roots more than necessary. Shake off the excess soil and study where the basic divisions should be. You might be able to break the clump with your hands — if the clump is too tough for this technique then use two hand forks or garden forks. Push the forks back-to-back into the centre and prise gently apart. Treat the resulting divisions in a similar fashion or tear apart with the fingers.

Select the divisions which came from the outer region of the clump — discard the central dead region of an old plant. Replant the divisions as soon as possible and water in thoroughly. Always check in the Flower Expert before lifting a perennial. Some dislike disturbance and some which can be moved may have a distinct preference for either autumn or spring.

RHIZOMES

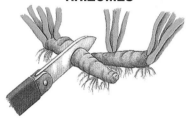

Carefully dig up the clumps of rhizomes — retain the roots. Divide up each rhizome into sections so that each piece bears leaves or buds above and roots below. Replant the sections at the same depth as the original plant. Summer is the usual time.

BULBS and CORMS

Clumps of most bulbs and corms need lifting and dividing every few years — the best time is when the foliage has died down. Lift with a fork and separate with your fingers. Replant large specimens at once in a spot where a display is required next year but plant the small offsets (bulblets or cormlets) 2-4 in. (5-10 cm) deep in an out-of-the-way spot. Leave undisturbed until they reach flowering size — then move to a display part of the garden.

Plants for a container

PLANTS FOR PERMANENT PLANTING

Dwarf Berberis	Hebe
Dwarf Conifers	Hedera
Erica	Lysimachia
Euonymus fortunei	Miniature Roses
Glechoma	Vinca

PLANTS FOR SEASONAL PLANTING

Alyssum	Dwarf Lathyrus
Dwarf Antirrhinum	Lobelia
Begonia	Mesembryanthemum
Bellis	Mimulus
Dwarf Bulbs	Pelargonium
Campanula isophylla	Petunia
Cineraria	Polyanthus
Convolvulus	Salvia
Dianthus	Tagetes
Fuchsia	Thunbergia
Gazania	Tropaeolum
Helichrysum	Universal Pansy
Impatiens	Verbana

Plants for a hanging basket

Asarina	Heliotropium
Asteriscus	Impatiens
Begonia	Lantana
Bellis	Dwarf Lathyrus
Brachycome	Lobelia
Calceolaria	Lotus
Calendula	Mimulus
Campanula	Nemesia
Chlorophytum	Nierembergia
Cineraria	Osteospermum
Coleus	Pelargonium
Convolvulus	Petunia
Dianthus	Phlox
Diascia	Portulaca
Euonymus fortunei	Scaevola
Felicia	Tagetes
Fuchsia	Thunbergia
Gazania	Tradescantia
Glechoma	Tropaeolum
Hedera	Verbana
Helichrysum	Viola & Pansy

House plant design terms

THE GOLDEN RATIO

This term is used by designers to describe the ratio 1 to 1.618 — it has been used since the time of Ancient Greece to create visually pleasing effects in buildings, paintings, landscaping, room design etc. About 2500 years ago it was found that this ratio was the basis of many of the proportions found in the human body, and later it was found that it applied to flowers, trees, shells and so on. And so it was applied to art — the relationship of the width to the length of the Parthenon in Athens follows the Golden Ratio, and so do many of the features in paintings from the 14th to the 21st century.

In roomscaping we can use a simplified version of this formula, which has been given many names including the Golden Mean, Golden Rectangle, Divine Proportion and the Golden Section. In simple terms it means that if a plant is $1\frac{1}{2}$ times taller than its neighbour, then the effect will be pleasing to our inner designer eye. If you are covering an area of wall with plants, try to aim for a rectangle with one side $1\frac{1}{2}$ times longer than the other. This is sometimes called the Goldilocks effect because of its not-too-little, not-too-much feel, but it is not a Golden Rule. There are times when a much more dramatic ratio is preferable.

Rock garden designs

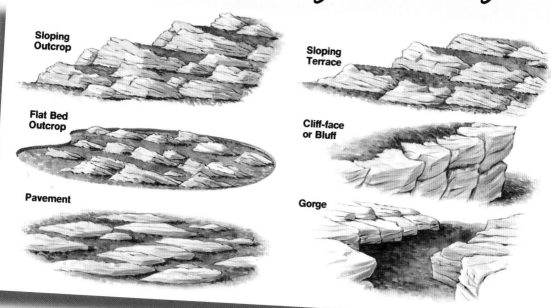

Sloping Outcrop

Sloping Terrace

Flat Bed Outcrop

Cliff-face or Bluff

Pavement

Gorge

Runner bean types

STICK varieties (S)

Nearly all runner beans will grow 8–10 ft high and bear pods which can reach 10–20 in. long. They are grown on tall supports and the usual flower colour is red. There is a bi-colour variety (Painted Lady) and the white and pink varieties are self-pollinating.

GROUND varieties (G)

A few Stick varieties can be sown 2 ft apart and grown as bushy plants by pinching out the growing point of the main stems when they are about 12 in. high. Side shoots are pinched out and the stems are supported by short twigs. The pods appear earlier than on climbing plants but there are disadvantages. The cropping period is short and pods are often curled and soiled.

DWARF varieties (D)

True Dwarfs are available — the plants grow 12–18 in. high and the pods are 6–8 in. long. They should be grown about 6 in. apart in rows 2 ft wide. A good choice where space is limited, but yields cannot compare with their climbing relatives.

Anatomy of a closeboard fence

Cap
A metal or wooden angled cover to protect end grain of the post from rain

Post
Ideally, this should be made of a rot-resistant timber such as cedar. Usually, however, it is a softwood pressure-treated with a preservative. Posts are set 8–10 ft apart

Post support
Each post is set in either concrete or a metal spike Firm support is essential

Pale
Strip of wood nailed to the arris rails. Pales are usually feathered and are fixed with a ½ in. overlap. Make sure this overlap is the correct width before nailing down

Capping rail
Horizontal board to protect end grain of the pales from rain

Arris rail
Board, triangular in cross section, fixed between posts. Use 2 (4 ft high fence) or 3 (6 ft high fence). Attach to posts with metal arris brackets. Nail pales to each arris rail

Gravel board
Horizontal board to prevent the bottom of the pales from rotting. This board and not the pales should touch the ground

Pales are butted (edge-to-edge)
or
feathered (thinner at one edge and overlapped)

Caring for your slipper orchid

PAPHIOPEDILUM

Pronunciation: paff-ee-oh-**PED**-ee-lum

Common Name(s): Slipper Orchid

Abbreviation: Paph.

Growth Type: Sympodial

Natural Habitat: On the ground (occasionally on rocks and trees) in tropical and subtropical Asia

Ease of Cultivation: Popular hybrids are easy — some species are challenging

Flowering Season: Depends on type — a collection can be in bloom all year round

Light: Less light required than for most other orchids — shade from direct sunlight

Temperature: Cool, Intermediate or Warm conditions, depending on type

Watering: Year round. Compost should be kept moist, but never let it become waterlogged

Resting Period: Not needed, but reduce water and feeding in winter

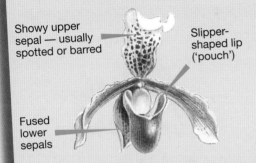

Typical Flower Form
Flowers borne singly or in small clusters on top of upright hairy spikes

Showy upper sepal — usually spotted or barred

Slipper-shaped lip ('pouch')

Fused lower sepals

Paphiopedilum insigne

Tulip colours

NORMAL TULIPS
No complex patterning

Self-coloured
(single colour throughout)

Blended
(one colour gradually merged with another)

Bi-coloured
(two distinct colours)

BROKEN TULIPS
Complex patterning caused by a virus

Feathered
(fine lines at edges)

Flamed
(feathered, plus central band)

Streaked
(bands along the petals)

Choosing plants

GOOD SIGNS

Pot-grown plant

BAD SIGNS

Clear labelling

Wilted leaves

Healthy and firm top-growth

Dry soil

Long roots growing through drainage holes

Germination facts

Plant	Germination Temperature	Germination Time (Days)
Ageratum	65°-70°F (18°-21°C)	10-14
Alyssum	60°-65°F (15°-18°C)	14
Antirrhinum	60°-65°F (15°-18°C)	10-21
Begonia, Fibrous-rooted	65°-70°F (18°-21°C)	14-21
Callistephus	65°-70°F (18°-21°C)	10-14
Dahlia, Bedding	65°-70°F (18°-21°C)	14-21
Dianthus	60°-65°F (15°-18°C)	14-21
Impatiens	70°-75°F (21°-24°C)	21
Lobelia	65°-70°F (18°-21°C)	21
Marigold & Tagetes	65°-70°F (18°-21°C)	7-14

Plant	Germination Temperature	Germination Time (Days)
Matthiola	65° (18°C)	10-14
Mesembryanthemum	65°-70°F (18°-21°C)	14-21
Mimulus	65°-70°F (18°-21°C)	14-21
Nemesia	65°-70°F (18°-21°C)	14-21
Pelargonium	70°-75°F (21°-24°C)	7-21
Petunia	70°-75°F (21°-24°C)	7-14
Phlox	60°F (15°C)	14-21
Salvia	70°-75°F (21°-24°C)	14-21
Verbena	65°-70°F (18°-21°C)	21-28
Zinnia	65°-70°F (18°-21°C)	7-14

Flower head types

SPIKE
Stalkless or almost stalkless flowers borne on the stem

RACEME
Like a Spike, but flowers are borne on short stalks

PANICLE
Like a Raceme, but each stalk bears a miniature Raceme

CORYMB
A flattened flower head — stalks arise from different points and the youngest flowers are at the centre

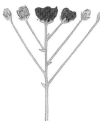

CYME
A flower head usually domed or flattened — stalks arise from different points and the oldest flowers are at the centre

CAPITULUM
A flattened flower head — stalkless flowers tightly packed together on top of a single disc

UMBEL
A domed or flattened flower head — stalks arise from a single point and the youngest flowers are at the centre

Bed or border?

Unfortunately there are no universally agreed definitions for 'bed' and 'border' and some attempts provide only a vague dividing line between the two. The definitions given below do give a clear-cut distinction between bed and border and are the meaning of the two terms used in this book.

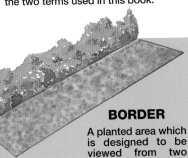

BORDER
A planted area which is designed to be viewed from two or three sides. Any shape, but usually rectangular.

BED
A planted area which is designed to be viewed from all sides. Any shape, but usually square, round or oval.

Flower arranging styles : 3

The LINE-MASS Style

Some open space is present within the boundary of the arrangement — only part of the area between the framework of line material is filled with leaves and/ or flowers. The period between 1950 and 1965 was an exciting time for flower arranging. The pioneering work by people like Constance Spry and Julia Clements continued to popularise the idea that making a flower arrangement could be an artistically-satisfying experience and not just a way of bringing garden flowers indoors. Equally important was the appearance of floral foam which made possible for everyone the creation of impressive displays. In light of this rapidly-growing interest in arranging flowers, the marriage of the Western Mass style and the Line style from the East was inevitable.

Line-mass became an important concept — a style in which the skeleton formed by line material was clothed but not covered by other flowers and/or foliage. The early teachers set out guidelines but unfortunately these were regarded as rules, and so for many years geometric patterns were carefully reproduced. Dominant material was dutifully grouped at the base and filler material was used to ensure a neat transition between the various elements. Things have now loosened up — irregular designs are now popular. This style is excellent for natural arrangements … after all, the garden with its twiggy shrubs above the massed flowers in the border is really a Line-mass arrangement!

Anatomy of a rose bush

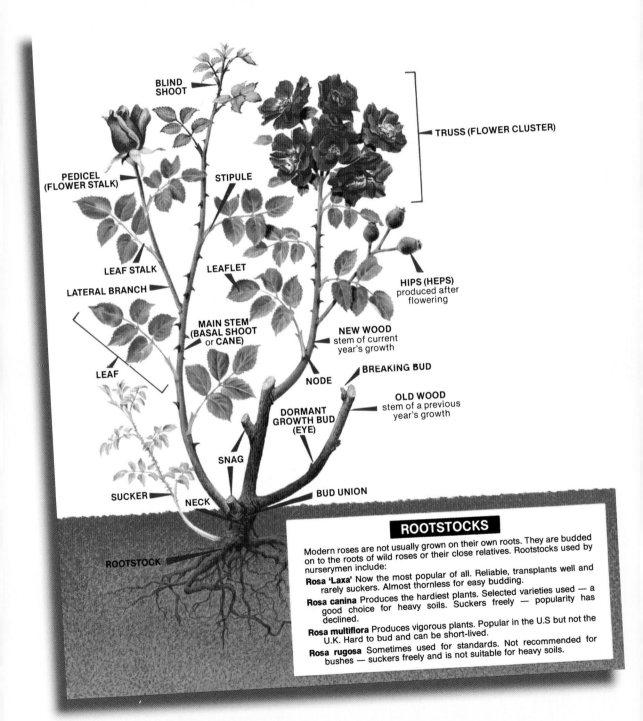

BLIND SHOOT

TRUSS (FLOWER CLUSTER)

PEDICEL (FLOWER STALK)

STIPULE

LEAF STALK

LEAFLET

LATERAL BRANCH

HIPS (HEPS)
produced after
flowering

MAIN STEM
(BASAL SHOOT
or CANE)

NEW WOOD
stem of current
year's growth

LEAF

BREAKING BUD

NODE

OLD WOOD
stem of a previous
year's growth

DORMANT
GROWTH BUD
(EYE)

SNAG

SUCKER   NECK

BUD UNION

ROOTSTOCK

ROOTSTOCKS

Modern roses are not usually grown on their own roots. They are budded on to the roots of wild roses or their close relatives. Rootstocks used by nurserymen include:

Rosa 'Laxa' Now the most popular of all. Reliable, transplants well and rarely suckers. Almost thornless for easy budding.

Rosa canina Produces the hardiest plants. Selected varieties used — a good choice for heavy soils. Suckers freely — popularity has declined.

Rosa multiflora Produces vigorous plants. Popular in the U.S but not the U.K. Hard to bud and can be short-lived.

Rosa rugosa Sometimes used for standards. Not recommended for bushes — suckers freely and is not suitable for heavy soils.

Butterfly or moth?

BUTTERFLY

Butterflies and moths are separated from all other insects by having scales on their wings. They have many similarities, especially in their life cycle, but there are enough points of difference to enable you to tell them apart.

MOTH

- Each antenna ends in a small knob
- All fly in the daytime
- Wings are usually brightly coloured
- Wings are nearly always held vertically when at rest

- Each antenna ends in a sharp point or fine 'feathers'
- Nearly all fly at night
- Wings are usually dull
- Wings are nearly always held horizontally when at rest

Making a patio bench

STEP 2:
SECURE THE SEATING
Use 2 planks of durable wood such as teak or cedar — pressure-treated softwood is a cheaper but less satisfactory alternative. Use rust-proof screws to secure the planks to the tops of the piers — butt the pieces of wood together

STEP 1:
ERECT THE PIERS
Make sure the base is firm and level. Build each pier using 6 courses of brick, as shown in the diagram. The 2 piers should be 4 ft apart

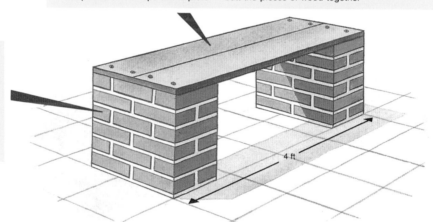

4 ft

Weed grasses in the lawn

HOLCUS LANATUS (Yorkshire fog)

POA ANNUA (Annual meadow grass)

A few native grasses occur as lawn weeds and can pose a problem — there is no chemical treatment. The first group of weed grasses consists of coarse-leaved species (e.g yorkshire fog) which form clumps. The answer is to dig out isolated patches and then reseed or returf — large areas should be slashed with an edging iron before mowing. The second type of weed grass is annual meadow grass. Not unsightly, but if the lawn grasses are weak it can take over the lawn in summer and it tends to die out in early autumn. Control measures include feeding the lawn in spring and using a grass box when mowing.

Choosing house plants

Plants for the south-facing window

ACACIA
ANIGOZANTHOS
BEDDING PLANTS
BOUGAINVILLEA
CACTI
CALLISTEMON
CELOSIA
CEROPEGIA
CHLOROPHYTUM
CITRUS
COLEUS
GERANIUM
GERBERA
GYNURA
HELIOTROPIUM

HIBISCUS
HIPPEASTRUM
HYPOCYRTA
IMPATIENS
IRESINE
JASMINUM
KALANCHOE
LANTANA
NERIUM
PASSIFLORA
PELARGONIUM
ROSA
SANSEVIERIA
SUCCULENTS
ZEBRINA

Lobivia hertrichiana

Callistemon citrinus

Plants for the east- and west-facing window

AECHMEA
AGLAONEMA
ANTHURIUM
APHELANDRA
BEGONIA
BELOPERONE
BILLBERGIA
CALADIUM
CALATHEA
CAPSICUM
CHLOROPHYTUM
CHRYSANTHEMUM
COLEUS
CORDYLINE
CROTON

CUPHEA
FICUS ELASTICA
GARDENIA
GYNURA
HOYA
IMPATIENS
NERTERA
POINSETTIA
SAINTPAULIA
SANSEVIERIA
SINNINGIA
SOLANUM
SPATHIPHYLLUM
TRADESCANTIA
ZEBRINA

Chrysanthemum morifolium

Caladium hortulanum

Plants for the north-facing window

AGLAONEMA
ANTHURIUM
ASPARAGUS
AZALEA
BEGONIA REX
BROMELIADS
CHLOROPHYTUM
COLUMNEA
CYCLAMEN
DIEFFENBACHIA
DIZYGOTHECA
DRACAENA
FUCHSIA

GARDEN BULBS
HEDERA
MARANTA
MONSTERA
PEPEROMIA
PHILODENDRON
PILEA
SANSEVIERIA
SCHEFFLERA
SCHLUMBERGERA
SCINDAPSUS
SPATHIPHYLLUM
VINES

Pilea cadierei

Tulipa greigii

Aubergine – Bambino – Black Enorma **Brussels sprout** – Rubine **Cabbage** – Red Drumhead – Ruby Ball **Capsicum** – Gypsy – Redskin **French bean** – Kinghorn Wax – Purple Podded	**Globe artichoke** **Leaf beet** – Ruby Chard – Swiss Chard **Lettuce** – Lollo Rossa **Rhubarb** **Runner bean** – Hestia – Painted Lady – White Lady **Tomato** – Yellow Perfection

Colourful vegetables

Winter protection of evergreens

In winter deciduous plants are devoid of foliage, so there is no water loss to dry out the tissues — in addition there are no leaves to be damaged by wind, rain, frost or snow. The situation is different with evergreens. Most established ones can quite happily withstand the rigours of winter, but others may be susceptible to damage and so need some form of protection.

Newly-planted conifers and leafy evergreen shrubs are most at risk, and it is the drying effect of strong winds which is more likely than frost to be the cause of browning or death in winter. The easiest answer is to plant in a spot which has the protection of other plants or a wall — failing that a screen as shown below may be necessary. Heavy frosts can be a problem with plants which are not completely hardy and a mulch will help — snow can cause damage with large leafy trees and tying up is sometimes needed.

SNOW PROTECTION

Plants most at risk: Cordyline, fir, cedar, cypress

The weight of snow on large conifer branches can cause them to break — if heavy snow is forecast it may be worth tying the branches of a choice evergreen or leafy palm-like plant with twine

In most cases all that is required is to knock off the snow from the branches with a cane — start at the bottom and work up

FROST PROTECTION

Plants most at risk: Evergreens which are not fully hardy

Cover the ground under the branches from December to early March with a 6 in. (15 cm) layer of leaves, bark or straw. Hold it down with netting or twigs

WIND PROTECTION

Plants most at risk: Newly-planted conifers and shrubs

Top of netting should be above the plant

Anchor stout posts firmly in the ground

Use windbreak netting or hessian — solid plastic sheeting is not recommended. Leave a 4 in. (10 cm) gap between plant and netting

Pin down base of netting

Small plants can be protected by draping horticultural fleece or placing a cloche over them

RAIN PROTECTION

Plants most at risk: Delicate evergreen rock garden plants

Place a sheet of rigid transparent plastic or glass over the plant on bricks. Secure with additional bricks. The top of the plant should not touch the surface. Remove when the weather turns mild in spring

If there are numerous plants to protect use cloches with open ends

Artificial flowers

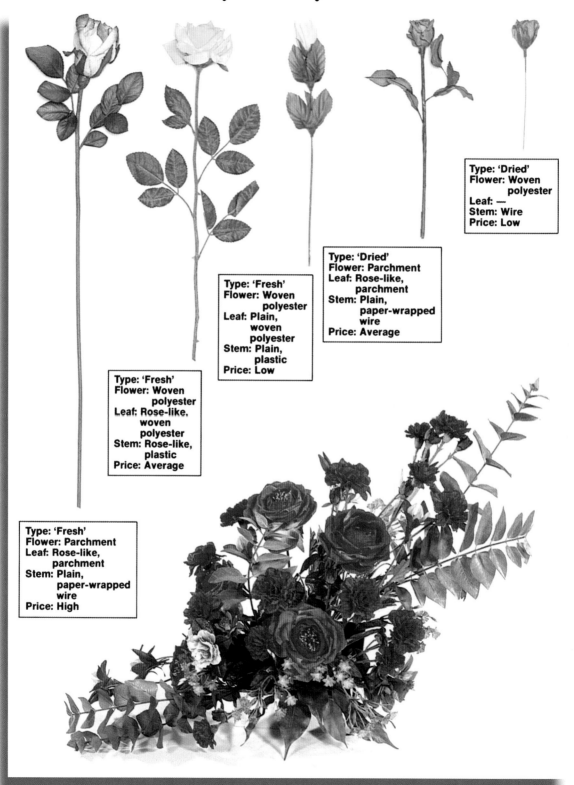

Type: 'Dried'
Flower: Woven
        polyester
Leaf: —
Stem: Wire
Price: Low

Type: 'Dried'
Flower: Parchment
Leaf: Rose-like,
        parchment
Stem: Plain,
        paper-wrapped
        wire
Price: Average

Type: 'Fresh'
Flower: Woven
        polyester
Leaf: Plain,
        woven
        polyester
Stem: Plain,
        plastic
Price: Low

Type: 'Fresh'
Flower: Woven
        polyester
Leaf: Rose-like,
        woven
        polyester
Stem: Rose-like,
        plastic
Price: Average

Type: 'Fresh'
Flower: Parchment
Leaf: Rose-like,
        parchment
Stem: Plain,
        paper-wrapped
        wire
Price: High

The 4-step planting plan

Make up the planting mixture in a wheelbarrow on a day when the soil is reasonably dry and friable – 1 part topsoil, 1 part moist leafmould or compost and 3 handfuls of bone meal per barrow load. Keep this mixture in a shed or garage until you are ready to start planting. Planting can take place at any time of the year, but the soil must be neither frozen nor waterlogged.

2 Water the pot or container thoroughly at least an hour before planting. Remove the plant very carefully – do not disturb the soil ball. With a pot-grown plant place your hand around the crown of the plant and turn the pot over. Gently remove – tap the sides with a trowel if necessary.

3 Examine the exposed surface – cut away circling or tangled roots but do not break up the soil ball. Fill the space between the soil ball and the sides of the hole with planting mixture. Firm down the planting mixture with your hands.

1 The hole should be deep enough to ensure that the top of the soil ball will be about 3 cm below the soil surface after planting. The hole should be wide enough for the soil ball to be surrounded by a layer of planting mixture (see above). Put a 3 cm layer of the planting mixture at the bottom of the hole.

4 After planting there should be a shallow water-holding basin. Water in after planting.

Cleaning out a small pond

There are several reasons why it may be necessary to clean out the pond. It may be leaking, the water may be polluted or there may be a thick layer of silt and rotting organic matter at the bottom.

Spring or summer is the time for this work. The first job is to make a temporary pool out of plastic or butyl sheeting in a shady spot — fill with pond water. Lift the marginal plants and the deep-water ones and put them in the temporary pool — now remove the floaters and oxygenators and put them in water-filled buckets or the temporary pool.

Begin to pump out the water. When shallow enough net the fish and place in a separate temporary pool — cover with fine netting. Finish draining the pond — lift up and divide any plants growing in the mud.

Remove the sludge layer and dump on vacant ground. Scrub the sides or use a pressure sprayer to remove the algae, taking care not to damage the surface. Refill the pond using tap water and replace the baskets of plants. After 3 or 4 days return the fish.

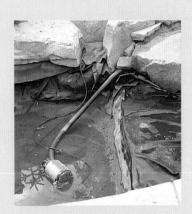

Germination facts

Plant	Germination Temperature	Germination Time (days)
Ageratum	65°-70°F (18°-21°C)	10-14
Alyssum	60°-65°F (15°-18°C)	14
Antirrhinum	60°-65°F (15°-18°C)	10-21
Aster	65°-70°F (18°-21°C)	10-14
Begonia, Fibrour-rooted	65°-70°F (18°-21°C)	10-21
Carnation	60°-65°F (15°-18°C)	10-21
Cineraria	70°F (21°C)	10-21
Dahlia, Bedding	65°-70°F (18°-21°C)	10-21
Dianthus	60°-65°F (15°-18°C)	10-21
Impatiens	70°-75°F (21°-24°C)	21
Lobelia	65°-70°F (18°-21°C)	21

Plant	Germination Temperature	Germination Time (days)
Marigold & Tagetes	65°-70°F (18°-21°C)	7-14
Mesembryanthemum	65°-70°F (18°-21°C)	14-21
Mimulus	65°-70°F (18°-21°C)	14-21
Nemesia	65°-70°F (18°-21°C)	14-21
Pelargonium	70°-75°F (21°-24°C)	7-21
Petunia	70°-75°F (21°-24°C)	7-14
Phlox	60°F (15°C)	14-21
Salvia	70°-75°F (21°-24°C)	14-21
Stock	65°F (18°C)	10-14
Verbena	65°-70°F (18°-21°C)	21-28
Zinnia	65°-70°F (18°-21°C)	7-14

Bonsai shapes

FORMAL UPRIGHT

INFORMAL UPRIGHT

TWIN TRUNK

SLANTING

WINDSWEPT

WEEPING

CASCADE

SEMI-CASCADE

ROOT-OVER-ROCK

Name that flower

Summer bedding plant
•
Hardy annual
•
Colours available

•
Flowering period

JANUARY
FEBRUARY
MARCH
APRIL
MAY
JUNE
JULY
AUGUST
SEPTEMBER
OCTOBER
NOVEMBER
DECEMBER

If your flower bed is in an open sunny situation and the soil drains freely then this unusual variety is well worth considering. It makes a welcome change from the usual range of low-growing annuals and the fragrant upturned bells are attractive to bees. The freely-branching stems bear hairy narrow leaves and throughout the summer the long-lasting blooms appear in large numbers. Staking is not needed — do not water unless the weather is very dry.

Answer on page 128

Trowels & hand forks

The **trowel** is a basic garden tool, essential for planting specimens too small for a spade. It is also used for digging out perennial weeds when minimal soil disturbance is required. The large range available makes choosing difficult, so a few simple rules are necessary. Buy stainless steel if you can afford it, avoid types with channelled blades in which earth can collect, make sure the handle is comfortable and buy two — one of standard size and the other a small narrow type with a blade about 2 in. across. Look for a strong neck and don't buy a long-handled one unless you find bending difficult.

Hand forks are about the same width as trowels, but bear 3–5 short tines instead of a scoop-like blade. They are used for weeding and cultivating soil around plants — buy a long-handled version to reach to the back of the border. The tines are available in various forms — flat, curved and twisted. Choose a fork with flat tines — the other shapes have drawbacks. The hand fork, unlike the trowel, is not essential.

The garden thicket

A garden thicket is a woody area which is planted primarily with native species and is arranged in several layers. First of all there are the trees if you have room, below which are the shrubs and then the wildflowers. At the base is the litter — a layer of dead leaves, twigs etc. Most gardeners do not have room for full grown trees and shrubs, so it is quite usual to trim the larger specimens. In this way a mixed hedge is produced.

The garden thicket is a haven for wildlife. Hedgehogs and mice nest in the surface litter. Birds, bees and butterflies gather around the flowers, seeds and berries. Leaves serve as food and nesting material for animal types which shun the 'foreign' fare offered by garden plants.

Try not to disturb the garden thicket — cleaning it up will frighten away some of the wildlife. However, some work is necessary for the first couple of years. Water in dry weather during the first year after planting and prune back the shoots during the first winter so that bushy growth will be encouraged. Mulch with bark and old leaves for 2 or 3 years.

Trees & Shrubs
Alder
Birch
Blackthorn
Dog Rose
Dogwood
Elder
Guelder Rose
Hawthorn
Hazel
Holly
Maple
Rowan

Climbers and Wildflowers
Bluebell
Crane's-bill
Foxglove
Hart's-tongue Fern
Honeysuckle
Ivy
Lily of the Valley
Old Man's Beard
Primrose
Snowdrop
Solomon's Seal
Violet
White Campion

Rogues gallery

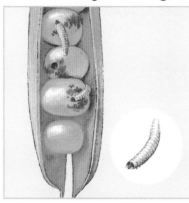

PEA MOTH

Maggoty peas are a familiar problem. The 8 mm yellowish caterpillars burrow through the pods and into the peas, making them unusable. The best way to avoid trouble is to sow a quick-maturing variety either early or late in the season. There are no suitable insecticides which can be relied upon for effective control.

Fixing window boxes

The preferred method of attachment will depend on the type of sill and window. You must choose one of the techniques illustrated below.

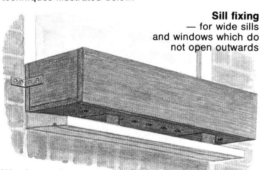

Sill fixing
— for wide sills and windows which do not open outwards

Wooden wedges are used to level the box on the sloping sill and to allow water to drain away. Angle brackets secure the box to the wall

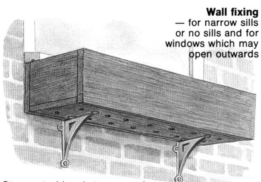

Wall fixing
— for narrow sills or no sills and for windows which may open outwards

Strong steel brackets are used to support the box — make sure screws and wall fixings are large enough for the weight to be carried. Also screw the back of the box to the wall

Making a bromeliad tree

Leafy Bromeliad —
Choose plants with a well pronounced 'cup' in the heart of the rosette. Remove from pot, wrap roots with sphagnum moss and then tightly attach with plastic-covered wire to branch

Tillandsia usneoides (Spanish Moss) — a unique Bromeliad which grows as grey-green strands in moist air. No watering required

Keep cup filled with water and spray sphagnum moss with water at weekly intervals

Branch set in Plaster of Paris and stones

Pebbles

Leafy Bromeliad

Sphagnum moss

Container

House plant miscellany

In the beginning: ORANGES & LEMONS

The story of growing frost-sensitive plants indoors began in Britain in the 16th century with the introduction of the orange tree. Rows of these trees became fashionable in the grand estates in the 17th century, and the large tubs were moved into a "house of defence" between October and April. At first these winter quarters were wooden buildings with few windows and charcoal-burning stoves as shown above. By the 18th and 19th centuries they had developed into the palatial glass orangeries to be seen at stately homes such as Sezincote, Woburn Abbey and Ham House. Sweet and seville oranges were the favourites — lemons were less popular.

Oranges are of course still grown for outdoor display in the summer garden with a winter rest in a conservatory. A popular approach for the house plant grower is to change things over — a dwarf variety such as calamondin orange (Citrofortunella mitis) is housed indoors for its near year-round display of flowers and fruit, with a spell outdoors in summer for fresh air and recuperation. The small fruit on the dwarf bushy tree is too bitter to eat, although it is suitable for making marmalade. The sweet orange (Citrus sinensis) needs greenhouse conditions for fruit production. For fruit you can use when grown under house plant conditions, try the lemon Citrus limon meyeri.

SPOTS

There is no single cause for spots on leaves. You should look at the colour and texture of the spots in order to find the reason for the trouble.

Mid brown, dry and crisp — too little water

Dark brown, dry and soft — too much water

White or straw coloured, dry — cold water on leaves or too much sun

Moist and/or sunken — pest or disease damage

Zantedeschia aethiopica

A YELLOW CARD FOR WHITEFLY

Whitefly can be a menace in the conservatory. They can be numerous enough to form a cloud over some ornamentals and they can be persistent enough to be present throughout the year. Unfortunately they are also remarkably resistant to chemical treatment — even regular repeat spraying will not completely eliminate them. A simple control method is to hang up one or more sticky yellow cards which are available from garden centres and DIY superstores. Whiteflies and some other flying insects such as greenflies and thrips are attracted by bright yellow — the surface glue holds them like old-fashioned fly paper.

Vertical bedding

The height of bedding-out skill or the ultimate in bad taste — both views have been expressed on vertical bedding. It all began in the early 1900s as a development of the carpet bed idea — 3-dimensional beds began to appear in public parks.

A piece of sculpture was made out of wire netting and filled with soil — flower vases and crowns were the most popular designs. The surface was then carpet-bedded and dot plants were placed around the base to form a piece of living sculpture. These beds were regarded with interest by the park visitors but the horticultural world did not like this odd approach — these sculptured beds died out nearly everywhere after the First World War. Exceptions are the Priory Gardens in Bath where nursery rhyme schemes are created each year and the Chelsea Flower Show where 3-D bedding displays have been a feature for many years.

Until recently vertical bedding had no practical use and certainly did not have a place in the home garden. The advent of Impatiens as a popular bedding plant has changed the picture — compost-filled screens covered with this bedding plant can be seen in the streets of Switzerland and other Continental countries.

A version of this screen can be made as a garden feature. Drive four stout wooden stakes into the ground so that about 9 in. (22.5 cm) is below the surface and 2 ft (60 cm) above. Wrap plastic netting around the posts to form a mesh box — attach the netting to the posts with wire. Line the inside with black polythene and fill with potting compost — insert two 1-ft (30-cm) long cardboard tubes during this filling process. Cut small holes in the polythene and plant. Impatiens seedlings in early June.

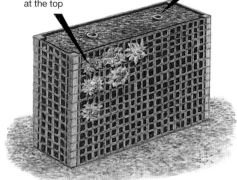

Plant with Impatiens to cover the surface of polythene at the sides and compost at the top

Water through tubes and over compost

Buying bedding plants

Good Signs

Compact sturdy stems with leaves near the base

Plants should be bushy and not packed too closely together. They should all be approximately the same size

The compost should be moist and there should be no sign of wilting leaves or drooping stems

Bad Signs

Plants in full flower. Abnormally early flowering is usually a sign of stress

Damaged or unlabelled container. Avoid trays, pots, strips etc which have been marked down for clearance

Lanky stems

Blemished, discoloured or diseased leaves

Roots growing through the base of the pot or tray

Pot plants are generally sold in flower. With strips and trays it is wise to buy plants in bud with just a few blooms open to show colour. Some bedding plants are nearly always in flower when bought — Mimulus, Impatiens, Bedding Begonia and French Marigolds are examples. Unless they are pot-grown avoid Geraniums and Petunias which are in flower.

Anatomy of a shed

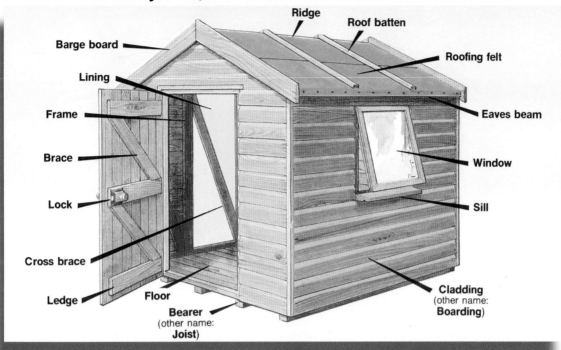

Ridge

Roof batten

Barge board

Roofing felt

Lining

Frame

Eaves beam

Brace

Window

Lock

Sill

Cross brace

Ledge

Floor

Cladding
(other name:
Boarding)

Bearer
(other name:
Joist)

Hints on hedging

Restoring a formal hedge

The popular quartet (yew, privet, box and laurel) can all be drastically cut back into old wood without coming to any harm. At the other end of the scale the conifers (except yew) will not sprout from pruned old wood.

The standard plan is to cut back one face of the hedge this season and then prune the other face next year. A flat top is acceptable if it is narrow — wide-topped hedges should be tapered so as to avoid snow damage.

The best time to prune is late winter for deciduous types and spring for evergreens. Feed and mulch in mid spring and water during dry weather. Gaps in the hedge can be filled in. Buy small plants — never try to match the height of the existing ones.

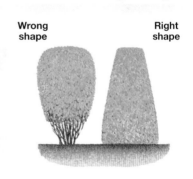

Wrong
shape

Right
shape

Starting from scratch

The first task is to decide the planting line. This needs some thought — right next to the pavement might seem a good idea, but there could be a serious overhang problem in years to come. Having decided on the line, dig out a 1 m wide strip. This trench should be 50 cm deep — put a layer of well-rotted manure or compost at the bottom. Single-row planting is acceptable if economy is necessary and quick screening is not, but double-row planting is recommended. After planting stretch wires tightly along the young plants and attach them to it with ties. Keep the plants watered during dry weather.

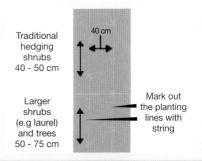

Traditional
hedging
shrubs
40 - 50 cm

40 cm

Larger
shrubs
(e.g laurel)
and trees
50 - 75 cm

Mark out
the planting
lines with
string

Motor-driven cultivators

Fuchsia types

A motorised cultivator seems like a good idea — a petrol-driven jack-of-all-trades to take the hard work out of gardening. Unfortunately it will not be of much help in the established ornamental garden. The main value of a motor-driven cultivator to the average gardener is the ability to dig over a large area when creating a new garden. If you are going to create a large vegetable garden as well as other features, then it is worth considering purchasing one of the many models available. If, however, the area is not large and most of the cultivated ground is to be turned into lawn and ornamental areas, it is a much better idea to hire one for the job of turning over the soil in your new garden. This will mean less work than digging, but it will also be less thorough. If you buy one there should be an adequate range of attachments — hoes, picks, ridgers, soil aerators etc.

There are 3 basic types. The most popular is the **mid-mounted rotor cultivator** — here the rotors are immediately below the engine and it is the preferred type for digging. Control is difficult when using it as a rotary cultivator. However, you can buy wheels to replace the rotor blades and fit a toolbar with attachments at the rear. Control is much easier when used in this way. The narrowest and generally lightest models are the **front-mounted rotor cultivators**. Here the motor blades are at the end of a boom at the front of the engine. These machines are easily handled, but they are for cultivating previously-dug ground rather than breaking up compacted soil. The final type is the **back-mounted rotor cultivator**. A fine machine to use, with power-driven wheels as well as a powerful rotor behind the engine. Unfortunately these are heavy machines with a price range (minimum £500) which puts them out of reach for the average gardener

SINGLE

F. 'Checkerboard'
F. 'Bon Accorde'
F. magellanica
F. 'Rufus'

SEMI-DOUBLE

F. 'Lady Thumb'
F. 'Snowcap'
F. 'Pink Flamingo'
F. 'Margaret'

DOUBLE

F. 'Alice Hoffman'
F. 'Blue Gown'
F. 'Swingtime'
F. 'Prosperity'

Do not feed plants with solid fertilizers right up to the stems. The feeding roots are some distance away from this region.

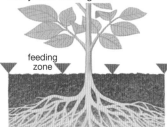

feeding zone

CLUSTERED

F. 'Thalia'
F. 'Mary'
F. 'Trumpeter'
F. 'Coralle'

Garden furniture types

| Garden chair | Director's chair | Tub chair | Tree seat | Bench | Hammock |

| Deck chair | Folding chair | Recliner | Sun lounger | Picnic table | Garden table |

House plant design terms

SHAPE, TEXTURE & PATTERN

These terms are used to describe the appearance of the foliage of a house plant. Shape covers the size and outline of the leaf, Texture is the physical nature of its surface and Pattern is the distribution of colour. Wander around the display at a large garden centre to see the range of Shapes — tiny-leaved mind-your-own-business to 50 cm-wide Monstera leaves, straight-edged Crotons to feathery asparagus fern. The range of Textures is equally wide — smooth, spiny, dull, shiny, velvety, ruffled etc. Finally, the patterns — all-green, variegated (green plus one other colour), multi-coloured, veined and so on. A mixture of Shapes, Patterns and Textures in your display will add interest, but a word of caution is necessary — too many different types in a feature can lead to confusion.

Mortar

Modern-day mortar is a mixture of cement and sand plus lime or a plasticiser.

● MIXES	Proportion by Volume			
	CEMENT	BUILDING SAND	HYDRATED LIME	PLASTICISER
MORTAR for bedding slabs and laying bricks and blocks	1 (Portland cement)	6	1	—
	or			
	1 (Portland cement)	6	—	Maker's instructions
	or			
	1 (Masonry cement)	5	—	—

Mortar has to be mixed on site — the best plan is to use the masonry cement/building sand mix if you have a large job to do or buy a bag of ready-mixed Bricklaying Mortar if you need only a small amount. A 25 kg bag will be needed for 50 bricks or 150 reconstituted stone blocks. It is important to add the right amount of water — it should hold the impression of the trowel, but it should not be watery nor should it be crumbly.

Prepare mortar on an old board. Dampen and then make a pile of half the sand. Add the other ingredients and then the rest of the sand. Mix these ingredients thoroughly. Build a heap, flatten the top and make a crater. Add some water to the crater and slowly bring the outer wall into the centre. Mix and turn — add sprinklings of water until the mortar is well mixed and properly moist.

Where orchids live

Nearly all of the orchids you will see are epiphytes, but a few important ones such as *Paphiopedilum* and *Phragmipedium* are ground dwellers.

EPIPHYTIC ORCHIDS

These plants grow on trees and may reach a great size. All are tropical or subtropical and are not parasitic. Roots grip the bark, and there are also fleshy aerial roots which take in moisture as well as nutrients derived from rotting plant litter and bird droppings.

LITHOPHYTIC ORCHIDS

These plants grow on bare rock or the mossy covering.

TERRESTRIAL ORCHIDS

These plants grow at ground level, usually in the surface layer of plant litter. All temperate orchids are terrestrial — the leaves die down in winter.

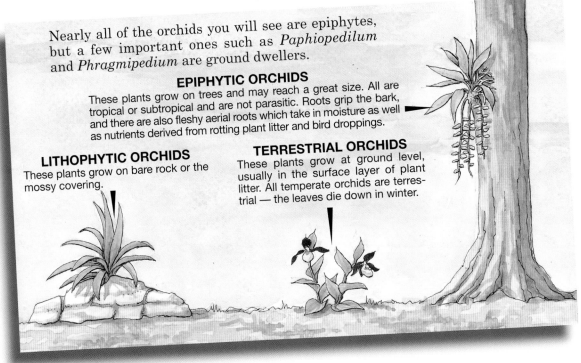

Topiary

Topiary involves the clipping of trees or shrubs into geometrical shapes and dates back to the Roman Empire. It can be used to create birds or animals on top of a hedge or yew figures on the lawn, but it is mostly used to produce green balls or cones in containers to flank a doorway.

There are two types of topiary. The major one uses evergreen shrubs which are densely clothed with leaves and can withstand regular clipping. The big three here are Buxus sempervirens (box), Taxus baccata (yew) and Laurus nobilis (bay). Others include Ilex, Juniperus, Ligustrum and Lonicera nitida. Simple shapes like cones can be cut freehand, but it is better to attach a framework of canes or wire to create the basic shape on to which the stems are tied. For complex shapes it is necessary to use a more complete frame made of stout wire and wire netting. In both cases trim back stem tips as they grow beyond the framework.

Once established the topiary tree or bush will need to be trimmed regularly. For a simple shape using yew an annual cut may be sufficient — at the other end of the scale a complex box topiary may need trimming every month during the growing season to maintain a manicured finish.

The second type of topiary uses leafy climbers. In warm regions several plants including Creeping Fig can be used, but in frost-prone countries Hedera (ivy) is the basic plant material. A frame of wire and wire netting is made to the desired shape and fixed firmly to the ground. Hedera is planted at intervals at the base of the frame and the stems are trained into the netting as they grow. Trim as necessary.

Lawn types

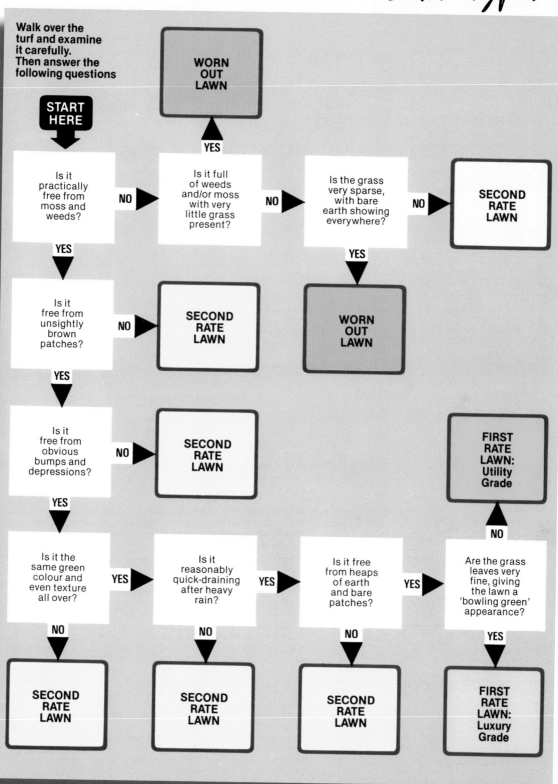

Walk over the turf and examine it carefully. Then answer the following questions

START HERE

WORN OUT LAWN

Is it practically free from moss and weeds?

NO → Is it full of weeds and/or moss with very little grass present?

YES ↑ WORN OUT LAWN

NO → Is the grass very sparse, with bare earth showing everywhere?

NO → SECOND RATE LAWN

YES ↓

Is it free from unsightly brown patches?

NO → SECOND RATE LAWN

YES ↓ WORN OUT LAWN

Is it free from obvious bumps and depressions?

NO → SECOND RATE LAWN

YES ↓

Is it the same green colour and even texture all over?

YES → Is it reasonably quick-draining after heavy rain?

YES → Is it free from heaps of earth and bare patches?

YES → Are the grass leaves very fine, giving the lawn a 'bowling green' appearance?

FIRST RATE LAWN: Utility Grade

NO ↓ SECOND RATE LAWN

NO ↓ SECOND RATE LAWN

NO ↓ SECOND RATE LAWN

YES ↓ FIRST RATE LAWN: Luxury Grade

NO ↑ FIRST RATE LAWN: Utility Grade

Planting a pond

STEP 1:
LINE THE BASKET
Use hessian — Finofil and louvred baskets do not need lining

STEP 2:
FILL THE BASKET
Use heavy loam from which twigs, roots etc have been removed. Do not add peat or compost — enrich with a little Bone Meal

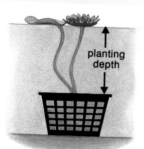

planting depth

STEP 4:
ADD GRIT LAYER
Place a 1 in. (2.5 cm) layer of pea shingle on top of the soil to prevent soil disturbance by fish

STEP 3:
PLANT UP THE BASKET
The correct time is between May and September — not in the dormant season. Firm planting is essential

STEP 5:
PUT THE BASKET IN THE POND
Water thoroughly. Deep-water aquatics should be introduced to the pond gradually. Stand the basket on a brick or two so that the crown is about 2 in. (5 cm) below the surface. Remove bricks as plants start to grow

Fruit tree shapes

Free-standing trees (bushes and standards) are the basic form – maintenance is usually straightforward once the framework has been established. A restricted form is used where space is limited. Such forms are grown against a fence or wall and are pruned in summer.

Trunk:
Standard
2–2.5 m
Bush
60–75 cm

Trunk:
Half standard
1–1.5 m
Dwarf bush
45–60 cm

BUSH
The **bush** and **dwarf bush** have short trunks and open centres. A dwarfing rootstock is used – aim to maintain a goblet-shaped framework. For planting in a large lawn there is the **half standard** – these trees are much more difficult to look after and cropping starts later.

PYRAMID
A **pyramid** is similar to a bush but a central leader has been maintained, giving a broadly conical shape. A variation (the **spindlebush**) has the side branches trained to grow horizontally. The **dwarf pyramid** is closely planted in rows. Summer pruning is necessary.

CORDON
A **cordon** is a single-stemmed tree which is planted at 45° and tied to a permanent support system such as a fence. Dwarfing rootstocks are generally used and very vigorous varieties are usually avoided. The ultimate height is about 1.5 m and several varieties can be grown together in a restricted space.

ESPALIER
The **espalier**, like the cordon, can be grown against a wall or fence. Its advantage is that it is more decorative than the cordon, but it also takes up more space and is more difficult to maintain. Buy trees which have already been trained.

FAN
The **fan**, like the espalier, is an attractive form when planted against a wall. It requires a large space – a height of 2 m and a spread of 3 m – and careful training is essential. Note that there is no central leader. Not popular for Apples – more widely used for Cherries and Peaches.

Repointing

Sooner or later the combined effects of wind, rain and frost will loosen some of the mortar between the bricks or blocks. The effect is unsightly and the weather resistance of the wall is reduced. Repointing of the affected area is the answer. Remove the loose mortar to a depth of about 1/2 in. with a screwdriver, a club hammer and cold chisel or an electric drill fitted with a chasing bit. Make up mortar from basic ingredients (page 107) or buy a bag of ready-mix — do not add too much water and incorporate some PVA bonding agent to increase its sticking properties. Never mix up more than you can use in an hour. Clear away all bits and dust with a stiff brush and then thoroughly soak the bricks and underlying mortar with water.

| FLUSH JOINT | RUBBED JOINT |
| WEATHER STRUCK JOINT | RECESSED JOINT |

Use a pointing trowel to force the mortar into the gaps — start with the upright joints and then fill the horizontal ones. Now smooth the mortar — cut away the excess and follow the joint style which has been used on the wall. For a rubbed joint use a small length of garden hose or a jointing tool. The final step is to brush off any traces of mortar when the repointed area is almost dry. These instructions are the standard ones you will find in any DIY manual, but they can lead to an unsightly patch if the whole wall is not repointed. It is a wise precaution to make up a small amount of mortar and repoint the gap between a brick or two before starting on the whole area. You may find that the new mortar when dry has quite a different colour to the rest of the jointing. You can buy colourants for mortar mixes — experiment until you find the right colour before repointing the whole area which requires treatment.

Reconstituted stone blocks are repointed in the same way as bricks. In recent years Mix 'n Point has appeared — this is a mortar mix which is applied directly from the bag to the space between the blocks — the strip of mortar is then smoothed with either a piece of cloth or a pointing trowel.

Orchid miscellany

The orchid in the kitchen

The Spanish Conquistadores found that the Aztecs used an extract of an orchid to flavour their cocoa drink. They named it **Vanilla** ('little pod'), and over the years it has been sold as an aphrodisiac and medicine as well as a flavouring agent. Several species are grown commercially for the vanillin extracted from the seed capsules, but the bottle on your kitchen shelf is likely to contain a synthetic substitute.

Name that shrub

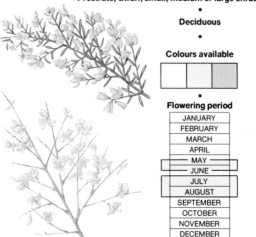

Prostrate, dwarf, small, medium or large shrub

Deciduous

Colours available

Flowering period

| JANUARY |
| FEBRUARY |
| MARCH |
| APRIL |
| MAY |
| JUNE |
| JULY |
| AUGUST |
| SEPTEMBER |
| OCTOBER |
| NOVEMBER |
| DECEMBER |

This group of Brooms have wiry stems, tiny leaves and a mass of yellow or golden flowers. All are sun-lovers and do best in light land, but the generalisations end there. There are spiny and thornless species, and heights range from 2 in. to 12 ft depending on the variety. The most popular types are the low-growing ones which can be used for covering dry banks or low walls. A key feature is the abundance of blooms — in the right conditions both leaves and stems are covered by the flowers. Do not feed — fertile soil reduces flowering.

Answer on page 128

Rogues gallery

VINE WEEVIL

These wrinkled white grubs are extremely destructive underground both outdoors and under glass. The roots of many plants may be attacked, but the favourite targets are alpines and plants growing in containers. If a plant suddenly dies, look in the soil for this rolled-up grub. Thiacloprid is a long-lasting preventative treatment.

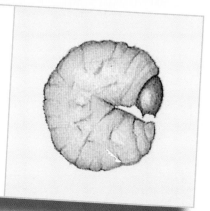

Conservatory or greenhouse?

There is no single feature which separates a conservatory from a greenhouse. A conservatory is usually a more ornate structure and is generally attached to the house wall, but there are exceptions — the great conservatories of the past were situated well away from the stately home. A green-house is generally a place where plants are raised and cultivated rather than set out for display — but greenhouses used solely for alpines or orchids illustrate that this feature has its exceptions.

The difference between these two types of plant house is a combination of several factors, and these are set out below.

THE CONSERVATORY	THE GREENHOUSE
The well-being and comfort of people are the prime consideration	The well-being and comfort of plants are the prime consideration
The basic purpose is the display of ornamental plants with showy leaves, stems and/or flowers	The basic purpose is the propagation and cultivation of plants which may or may not be ornamental
In most but not all cases the structure is attached to the house	In most but not all cases the structure is detached from the house
In most but not all cases the structure is decorative and with external ornamentation	In most but not all cases the structure is practical and without external ornamentation
Some form of decorative flooring is present, ranging from simple matting to marble tiles	Some form of practical flooring is present, such as compacted soil or concrete
Wood and uPVC are the favourite framing materials — glazing bars are usually sturdy	Aluminium is the favourite framing material — glazing bars are usually slender
A small but well-designed version is expensive	A small but well-designed version is relatively cheap

Troughs

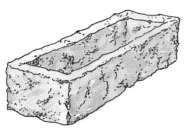

STONE TROUGH

Stone troughs are hard to find these days, but excellent reconstituted stone ones can be bought. Use for rock garden plants. An artificial stone trough can be made from a sink

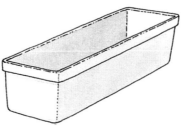

PLASTIC TROUGH

Shiny plastic troughs are widely available from garden centres and DIY stores. They are inexpensive and lightweight, but there are no other virtues. Cover surface with trailers to improve appearance

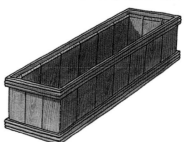

WOODEN TROUGH

A good choice, combining a natural appearance with a reasonable price. Many types are available including DIY ones, rustic faced troughs, hardwood and softwood, stained and painted

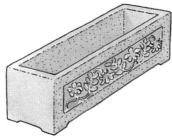

DECORATED TROUGH

Carved stone troughs are a feature of the grand garden, but are extremely expensive nowadays. An acceptable alternative is one of the reconstituted stone or fibreglass ones. Many patterns are on offer

METAL TROUGH

Antique lead, iron and copper containers are very expensive. You can find modern ones in traditional patterns which have been cast from lead, faux (false) lead and bronzage (bronze-resin compound)

Potato types

FIRST EARLY varieties

Potatoes grown for harvesting in June or July. These early-maturing varieties do not produce high yields, but they are ready when shop prices are high. They take up less space than Maincrops and are not subject to the ravages of blight. First Earlies are not generally grown for storage — lifting takes place when the tubers are quite small and they are treated as new potatoes for immediate cooking.

SECOND EARLY varieties

A small and declining group of potato varieties which bridge the gap between the First Earlies of July and the Maincrops of autumn. Sometimes called Mid-season varieties.

MAINCROP varieties

Potatoes grown for maximum yields of tubers — these potatoes are stored for winter use. Some lists separate Early Maincrops which are ready in early or mid September (Desirée, Maris Piper etc) from Late Maincrops (Golden Wonder etc) which are harvested in late September or October.

House plant miscellany

In the beginning: ORCHIDS

In 1731 the plant collector Peter Collinson received a dried plant from the Bahamas. He planted it and it grew — this was the first exotic orchid (Bletia verecunda) to flower in Britain. Another early arrival was Epidendrum cochleatum which crossed the Atlantic in 1786 and was the first tree-living orchid to flower in Britain. The beginning of the 19th century saw the start of the great orchid hunt — plant hunters scoured the tropical world for them and there was an enormous demand for this new status symbol. Prices were high as losses in cultivation were great — only slowly did growers realise that constantly hot and moist conditions were not only unnecessary but positively harmful. The first hybrid appeared in 1856 and for over a century these plants continued to be regarded as beautiful but rather 'special'. It was only at the end of the 20th century that the moth orchid began to appear in outlets everywhere as just another attractive house plant for everyone.

Cymbidium

DECORATIVE MULCHES

You will either love or hate decorative mulches which are placed on top of the compost in pots or other receptacles. They are a popular finishing touch for some designers when creating an indoor plant display — they certainly provide an additional texture and a new colour. It is claimed that they reduce water loss, but this is not a good thing for most plants as this moisture arising from the surface compost increases the air humidity around the leaves.

All sorts of material can be used — coloured glass beads, broken shells, white pebbles, polished stones, grit and dried moss. An exciting and attractive new feature or an offensive and unnatural way of spoiling a display — it is up to you, but before making up your mind you should remember that a surface cover will make the finger test more difficult.

Glass mulch

Shell mulch

Pruning roses

❀ MINIATURE ROSES • SHRUB ROSES • CLIMBERS

✗

Cutback Method

Don't cut these roses back like Hybrid Teas or Floribundas — very little pruning is required.

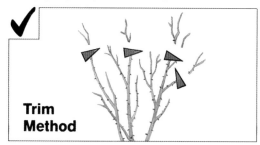

✓

Trim Method

Cut off dead and sickly growth and then merely trim to shape if necessary to avoid overcrowding.

❀ PATIO ROSES • HYBRID TEAS • FLORIBUNDAS

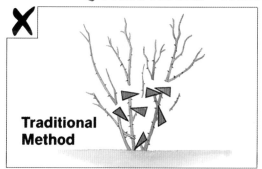

✗

Traditional Method

The first step is to remove all dead, diseased and damaged wood, and then cut out weak and soft growth. Congested stems in the centre of the bush are removed and finally the remaining healthy stems are dealt with. Each shoot is cut back, using a sloping cut close to an outward-facing bud. The amount removed is $1/3$–$2/3$ of the shoot, depending on the rose type.

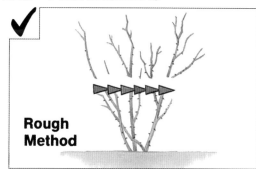

✓

Rough Method

Nothing could be simpler — the bush is cut to half its height with secateurs or a hedge trimmer. Leave all the weak and twiggy growth. Cut out dead wood to the base if you want to. Surprisingly, bushes pruned by this method produce more and bigger blooms than roses cut back by the laborious Traditional Method recommended in the textbooks.

Holiday care for containers

Your time for rest and relaxation away from home in summer may be a time of decline or even death for your plants in containers. The most satisfactory solution is to persuade a friend to call and look after them. If you can't find a plant babysitter then you should create the illustrated set-up. Move the containers if you can to a shady spot and place a large bowl filled with water on some form of support above them. Run a length of wick, strip of capillary matting or other sort of absorbent cloth from the bottom of the bowl to the compost surface in each container — push the wick below the surface.

Why orchids die

TOO MUCH FERTILIZER
Two rules — do not feed when plants are not actively growing and do not exceed the recommended dose

DIRECT RADIANT HEAT
Orchids should never be placed in front of a radiator. Too much heat leads to leaf collapse

WET LEAVES
Leaves which are left wet overnight are a common cause of fatal disease. Water and mist early in the day

OVERWATERING
The main cause of death. Follow the watering rules — do not assume lack of water is the cause of all ills

COLD DRAUGHTS
Draughts are not the same as ventilation. Draughts involve the rapid movement of air between one opening and another

DRY & STUFFY AIR
Some method of increasing air moisture is needed for most orchids and so is air movement around the plant

STRONG SUMMER SUN
Too much sunlight leads to scorching heat. Some direct sun may be recommended, but shade from midday summer sun is always required

Tubs

HALF-BARREL
Wooden half-barrels are now specially made for use as plant containers. Plastic, reconstituted stone and fibreglass versions are also available

VERSAILLES TUB
The traditional container for Orange trees and topiary. Stained or painted wood is the standard material, but plastic and fibreglass ones can be bought

GERANIUM POT
A wide-mouthed container which is a tub rather than a pot. The distinctive feature is a series of narrow ridges around the terracotta surface. Good, but no longer popular

MODERN PLANTER
Clean, uncluttered and without ornament — a good choice in the right situation. The usual materials are plastic, concrete, fibreglass and reconstituted stone

TRADITIONAL PLANTER
The surface is textured or ornamented. Basic shapes are round, oval or square and the materials are stone, metal, terracota, plastic and reconstituted stone

QUADRANT PLANTER
A triangular container which can be used in various ways. The usual situation is in a corner, but four can be fitted together to form a large square for planting herbs etc

Mulching

A mulch is a layer of bulky organic matter placed on the soil surface around plants. Mulches are not applied around annuals, but around shrubs, trees and herbaceous perennials they provide several distinct benefits:

- The soil below is kept moist during the dry days of summer
- The soil surface is kept cool during the hot days of summer. This moist and cool root zone promotes more active growth than in unmulched areas
- Annual weeds are kept in check — the ones that do appear can be easily pulled out
- Some mulches provide plant foods
- Soil structure is improved by the addition of humus

Many materials are suitable for mulching — you can use pulverised bark, leaf mould, well-rotted manure, mushroom compost and garden compost. Grass clippings are sometimes recommended and are often used, but a word of caution is necessary. Add a thin layer and stir occasionally — do not use them if they are weedy or if the lawn has been treated with a weedkiller.

The standard time for mulching is May. Success depends on preparing the soil surface properly before adding the organic blanket. Remove debris, dead leaves and weeds, and then water the surface if it is dry. Apply a spring feed if this has not been done, hoe in lightly and you are now ready to apply the mulch. Spread a 2–3 in. layer over the area which is under the branches and leaves — do not take the mulch right up to the stems — a build-up of moist organic matter around the crown may lead to rotting. In October lightly fork this dressing into the top inch of soil — replace in spring. Autumn mulching is sometimes recommended as a way of preventing frost getting down to the roots, but it will increase the risk of dangerous air frosts around the plants in spring.

The benefits of using an organic mulch in the spring are remarkable, but it is still not generally practised. The use of black polythene sheeting as an inorganic mulch in the vegetable garden is even less popular, but its value can be outstanding. Strips of black plastic are laid across the prepared soil and the edges buried under the surface. Slits are cut in the surface to act as planting holes, and growth is stimulated by the moist conditions created. Potatoes do not need earthing up and Strawberries, Marrows, etc are kept off the ground. The greatest boon, however, is in weed-infested land as the plastic sheeting forms a weed-proof barrier.

Ogier Ghislain de Busbecq was the Austrian Emperor's Ambassador to Suleiman the Magnificent in the 16th century. He sent seeds and bulbs of the Tulip back to Vienna — a plant new to the European scene. The name he gave was an error — he based it on the word for turban rather than using its true Turkish name (lalé). Busbecq also introduced the Crown Imperial

Apple calendar

NOV	DEC	JAN	FEB	MAR	APR	MAY	JUN	JUL	AUG	SEP	OCT
PLANT — bare-rooted trees											
PLANT — container-grown trees											
PRUNE — all trees						PRUNE — supported types					
SPRAY — as required											
										PICK	
STORE										STORE	

Name that flower

Garden plant
•
Tuberous root
•
Colours available

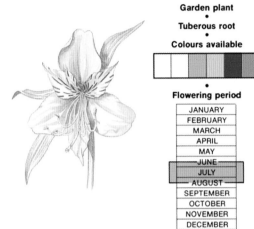

•
Flowering period

| JANUARY |
| FEBRUARY |
| MARCH |
| APRIL |
| MAY |
| JUNE |
| JULY |
| AUGUST |
| SEPTEMBER |
| OCTOBER |
| NOVEMBER |
| DECEMBER |

The 2 in. (5 cm) wide flowers are attractive, variously described as Lily-like, Azalea-like or Orchid-like. They are often streaked or spotted with darker colours and are borne in loose clusters. They are long-lasting in water and you will find them in your local florist, but you will not often see them in gardens. The problem is that few flowers are produced in the first year.

Answer on page 128

Orchid miscellany

The orchid that began it all

In 1826 the Governor of Trinidad brought plants of **Oncidium papilio** to England, and in 1833 specimens in bloom were exhibited at the Horticultural Society of London. The sixth Duke of Devonshire attended the show and was utterly captivated by the butterfly-like blooms.

He became an avid collector, and his enthusiasm for orchids slowly spread to wealthy landowners around the country. Collectors began to comb the tropics for new species, and this widespread interest steadily increased until it became the Orchidmania starting in the 1850s.

The butterfly orchid has changed its name to **Psychopsis papilio**, but its charm remains.

Pelargonium types

BEDDING GERANIUMS

Flowers ½-1 in. (1-2.5 cm) across. White, pink, salmon, red, purple

Rounded leaves; nearly all varieties having a horseshoe marking or 'zone'

P. hortorum

'Video Pink'

REGAL PELARGONIUMS

Flowers 1½-2 in. (3.5-5 cm) across. Frilled. White, pink, salmon, red, purple — usually marked with darker colour

Serrated leaves

P. domesticum

'Elsie Hickman'

IVY-LEAVED PELARGONIUMS

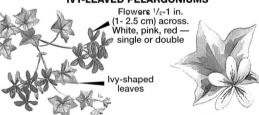

Flowers ½-1 in. (1- 2.5 cm) across. White, pink, red — single or double

Ivy-shaped leaves

P. peltatum hybrid

'L'Elegante'

ANGEL GERANIUMS

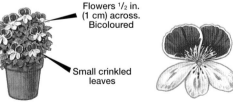

Flowers ½ in. (1 cm) across. Bicoloured

Small crinkled leaves

P. crispum hybrid

'Captain Starlight'

Pond balance

Each of the components of the pond — water, plant life, soil, fish and dead organic matter must be balanced so that the growth of algae is inhibited.

The first need is to keep down the amount of unwanted organic matter. Remove dead plants and fallen leaves, do not incorporate peat, compost or soluble fertilizers when potting up plants and do not give more food than the fish can eat in a short time. Next, provide some shade. Grow water lilies and/or other plants so that half the surface is covered. The third basic need is to deprive the algae of the carbon dioxide and minerals which are essential for their development. This task is performed by the oxygenators — lowly underwater plants which play a vital role in keeping the water clear. They also supply oxygen which is utilised by the fish. Pond size is a critical factor — even if you do all the recommended things it will still be impossible to achieve proper balance in a pond of less than 4 sq.m.

Your pond will always turn cloudy and slightly green in spring, but with proper balance it will soon clear once active plant growth begins.

Forks

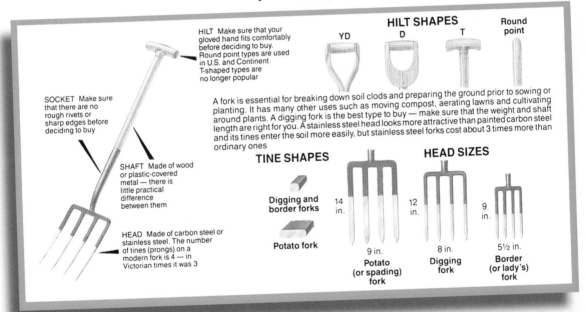

HILT Make sure that your gloved hand fits comfortably before deciding to buy. Round point types are used in U.S. and Continent. T-shaped types are no longer popular

HILT SHAPES

YD   D   T   Round point

SOCKET Make sure that there are no rough rivets or sharp edges before deciding to buy

A fork is essential for breaking down soil clods and preparing the ground prior to sowing or planting. It has many other uses such as moving compost, aerating lawns and cultivating around plants. A digging fork is the best type to buy — make sure that the weight and shaft length are right for you. A stainless steel head looks more attractive than painted carbon steel and its tines enter the soil more easily, but stainless steel forks cost about 3 times more than ordinary ones

SHAFT Made of wood or plastic-covered metal — there is little practical difference between them

TINE SHAPES

Digging and border forks

Potato fork

HEAD SIZES

14 in.   12 in.   9 in.

9 in.   8 in.   5½ in.

Potato (or spading) fork   Digging fork   Border (or lady's) fork

HEAD Made of carbon steel or stainless steel. The number of tines (prongs) on a modern fork is 4 — in Victorian times it was 3

Replacing old roses

Roses generally fail to thrive when planted in soil which has grown the same or a different variety for 10 years or more. This is because the new plant becomes affected by replant disease — a complex soil problem which is caused by the previous rose. There is no known cure.

If you plan to replace an old rose you should buy a container-grown and not a bare-root plant. Remove the old soil, digging out a hole which is 60 cm across and about 50 cm deep. Mix in plenty of compost with the soil in the bottom of the hole. Fill the space around the plant with soil from a part of the garden which has not grown roses. The old soil from the hole can be safely spread on flower beds or in the vegetable garden.

Weeds around growing plants

There are basically two types of products for use around growing plants. Weedkillers based on diquat act as a chemical hoe, killing the top growth of weeds within a few days. Quick-acting, but the roots are not harmed and so they are not effective against perennial weeds.

Glyphosate and glufosinate ammonium go down to the roots and so both perennial and annual weeds are killed. They are slower acting than diquat and may take several weeks to work. It may be necessary to repeat the treatment later in the season.

Both diquat and glyphosate will kill garden plants as well as weeds, so you must keep the spray away from the foliage of trees, shrubs, flowers, vegetables etc. Use either a ready-to-use spray gun or apply diluted spray from a watering can fitted with a dribble bar. Work as close to the weeds as possible. Never use weedkiller spraying equipment for any other purpose. Choose a still day when the weeds are actively growing in late spring or summer.

The most difficult situation is where the weeds are growing next to flowers and shrubs or twining up their stems. It is safer to apply glyphosate gel here rather than a spray, using **the glyphosate glove technique**. Put some of the weedkiller on the thumb and forefinger of a rubber glove and stroke the leaves. Bindweed can be a serious nuisance. Insert a cane well above the height of the plant and allow the weed to climb up it — treat as shown in the illustration on the left.

Pea types

ROUND varieties

The seeds of these varieties remain smooth and round when dried. They are all First Earlies — hardier and quicker-maturing than other types and more able to withstand poor growing conditions than the Wrinkled types. Round varieties are used for late autumn and early spring sowing.

WRINKLED varieties

The seeds of these varieties are distinctly wrinkled when dried. These 'marrowfat' peas are sweeter, larger and heavier cropping than the Round ones, and are therefore much more widely grown. They are, however, less hardy and should not be sown before March. These Wrinkled varieties are classified in two ways. Firstly by height (there are the $1\frac{1}{2}$–2 ft dwarfs and the 4–5 ft tall varieties) and secondly by the time taken from sowing to first picking. First Earlies take 11–12 weeks, Second Earlies 13–14 weeks and Maincrop 15–16 weeks. In catalogues and garden centres you will find a large choice from each group.

MANGETOUT varieties

There are several types included in this group — chinese peas, snow peas, sugar snaps and eat-all. They are rather easier to grow than garden peas — pick before the seeds swell and cook the pods whole.

PETIT POIS varieties

Petit pois are not immature peas gathered from small pods of any garden pea variety — they are a small number of dwarf varieties which produce tiny ($\frac{1}{8}$–$\frac{1}{4}$ in.) peas which are uniquely sweet.

ASPARAGUS PEA variety

This variety is also known as the winged pea. It is not really a pea at all — it is a vetch which produces sprawling bushy plants. It is not frost-hardy, so sowing must be delayed until May. The red flowers which appear in summer are followed by curiously shaped winged pods — these must be gathered whilst they are still small or they will be fibrous and stringy. The small pods are cooked whole like mangetout.

Watering overhead containers

It is easy to forget that small containers will need frequent watering in hot and dry weather. This is a time consuming but not difficult task in most cases, but it can be a problem with overhead containers such as hanging baskets and window boxes. It is possible to use steps and a watering can in some instances, but there are three alternatives which can make the task easier.

HOSE LANCE
Convenient with unlimited capacity — large areas can be covered. Difficult to direct accurately. Lances with fitted fertilizer applicators are now available

PUMP CAN
Neat and simple to use — no hose pipe is needed. Suitable if you have one or two hanging baskets to water but not practical for large areas

UP-DOWN MECHANISM
The basket is brought down to easy reach. Two types are available — a simple pulley on the bracket or a spring-loaded holder on the basket chain

Plum types

	DESSERT PLUM	CULINARY PLUM	GAGE
MATURE BUSH 15-25 ft high	Sweet — eaten fresh. Fleshy fruit — trees smaller and less hardy than culinary varieties. Most popular variety: *Victoria*	Rather tart — used for cooking. Fruit less fleshy than dessert varieties — trees more tolerant of poor conditions. Most popular variety: *Czar*	Smaller, rounder and sweeter than dessert Plums Yields are not high. Rather tender — grow as a fan against a south wall

	BULLACE	DAMSON	MIRABELLE
MATURE BUSH 10-15 ft high	Sharp flavour — used for cooking. Fruit left until late autumn before picking. Choose a Damson variety instead	Spicy tart flavour — used for cooking, jam- and wine-making. A hardy tree which succeeds where a Plum would fall	Similar in shape to Bullace, but sweeter and golden-yellow. Found in the textbooks but not in the catalogues

	MYROBALAN (CHERRY PLUM)	
MATURE BUSH 20-30 ft high	A decorative Plum used as a specimen tree and for hedging — attractive blossom in March. Cherry-like fruit in July which can be used for cooking or jam-making	

Rootstocks

The most widely used rootstock is **St Julien A** — this is the one to choose if conditions are less than ideal. A newer dwarfing form (**Pixy**) is becoming quite popular as it produces bushes with a mature height of only 10-15 ft. You do need good soil and good growing conditions for Pixy-rooted Plums — some nurserymen do not recommend this rootstock for northern districts.

Other stocks are available. **Myrobalan B** is far too vigorous for ordinary gardens. **Brompton** comes to fruit quickly and resists suckering, but it is much more vigorous than St Julien A. **Mussel** produces a more compact tree than either Myrobalan B or Brompton.

House plant dictionary

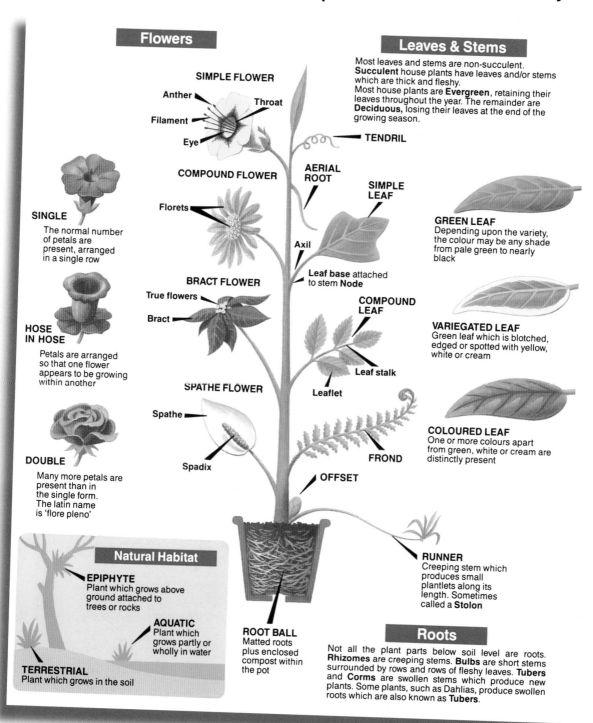

Flowers

SIMPLE FLOWER
- Anther
- Throat
- Filament
- Eye

COMPOUND FLOWER
- Florets

BRACT FLOWER
- True flowers
- Bract

SPATHE FLOWER
- Spathe
- Spadix

SINGLE
The normal number of petals are present, arranged in a single row

HOSE IN HOSE
Petals are arranged so that one flower appears to be growing within another

DOUBLE
Many more petals are present than in the single form. The latin name is 'flore pleno'

Leaves & Stems
Most leaves and stems are non-succulent. **Succulent** house plants have leaves and/or stems which are thick and fleshy.
Most house plants are **Evergreen**, retaining their leaves throughout the year. The remainder are **Deciduous,** losing their leaves at the end of the growing season.

- TENDRIL
- AERIAL ROOT
- SIMPLE LEAF
- Axil
- **Leaf base** attached to stem **Node**
- COMPOUND LEAF
- Leaf stalk
- Leaflet
- FROND
- OFFSET

GREEN LEAF
Depending upon the variety, the colour may be any shade from pale green to nearly black

VARIEGATED LEAF
Green leaf which is blotched, edged or spotted with yellow, white or cream

COLOURED LEAF
One or more colours apart from green, white or cream are distinctly present

RUNNER
Creeping stem which produces small plantlets along its length. Sometimes called a **Stolon**

Natural Habitat

EPIPHYTE
Plant which grows above ground attached to trees or rocks

AQUATIC
Plant which grows partly or wholly in water

TERRESTRIAL
Plant which grows in the soil

ROOT BALL
Matted roots plus enclosed compost within the pot

Roots
Not all the plant parts below soil level are roots. **Rhizomes** are creeping stems. **Bulbs** are short stems surrounded by rows and rows of fleshy leaves. **Tubers** and **Corms** are swollen stems which produce new plants. Some plants, such as Dahlias, produce swollen roots which are also known as **Tubers**.

Flower care in winter time

For the annuals there is no winter care — their life span is over. The half-hardy perennials must also leave the garden, but for them there is a stay indoors before being reintroduced into the garden with the return of frost-free weather in the spring. It is unwise to generalise about the proper conditions for half-hardy perennials and bulbs which must overwinter indoors. It is a period of rest during which bulbs are kept dry and cool whilst varieties overwintered as green plants are given just enough water to keep them alive.

Outdoors the border perennials, rockery perennials and hardy bulbs await the return of spring in the open ground. Most of them have nothing to fear. The snow and frost will do them no harm provided the soil does not become waterlogged — drowned roots kill more plants than frozen ones.

Late autumn is the usual time for cutting back the dead stems of border perennials. Do not cut down evergreens and winter-flowering plants, of course, and perennials which are not fully hardy should be cut down in spring.

Forking over is a traditional autumn technique but if you have put down a mulch in late spring you can leave it undisturbed until next year. Use a fork to break up the surface crust, turning over the top couple of inches of soil between the plants. Forking over is an enjoyable job to do on a sunny day in autumn, but it probably does you more good than the plants unless your soil is prone to severe crusting and mossing over.

Perennials which are not completely hardy present a problem. You can cover them with glass cloches but it is more usual to put a blanket of straw, bracken, leaf mould or peat over the crowns.

Delicate but hardy alpines need protection from winter rains rather than from frosts. The standard method is to cover the plants with a pane of glass supported by bricks.

Planting bulbs in tubs

STEP 2:
FINISH PLANTING
Sift compost between the bulbs and then add more of the planting medium so that a 1-2 in. (2.5-5 cm) watering space is left at the top of the container. There are two alternative techniques. In layer planting the addition of this compost stops at an earlier stage so that a layer of smaller bulbs can be added (for example Crocuses over Daffodils) in order to extend the display. Another variant is part planting — here the trees, shrubs and/or bedding plants are put in first and the bulbs are then planted with a trowel to the correct depth in the compost. Whichever technique you use the compost should be kept moist and the bulbs should be lifted when the display is over for later planting in the garden

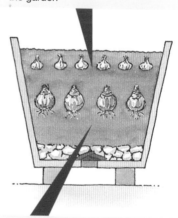

STEP 1:
BEGIN PLANTING
Prepare the container, put it in place and add a drainage layer as shown in the illustration above. Now add soilless potting compost, pressing down gently with your hands. Stop adding compost when the correct height is reached — which is when the bulbs placed on the layer will be covered with the recommended height of compost, measured from the tip of the bulb to the top of the growing medium. Buy bulbs which are large, firm and healthy — place them on the compost with little space (approximately 1 in.) between them

Lawn design

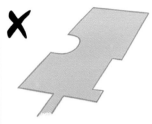 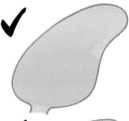

Round off sharp corners and smooth out tight curves — the outline should ideally be roughly oval or kidney-shaped. Grass paths and the strips between island beds and the edge of the lawn should be at least 3 ft (1 m) wide.

 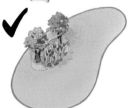

Avoid having a scatter of trees, shrubs and beds over the grass — they make the lawn look smaller and mowing becomes a long and tedious process. If it is possible group at least some of the plants together into a single large bed.

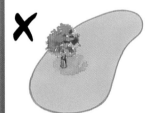 

If there are one or more trees already on the lawn do cut off the lower branches if they interfere with easy mowing. If you are planning to put in a tree then choose a spot elsewhere in the garden or at the side of the lawn.

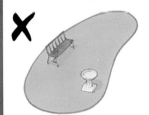 

Seats, pots, sundials etc are attractive features in a garden but they do not belong on the lawn if you want mowing to be as easy a task as possible. Site furniture elsewhere in the garden or on paving along the lawn edge.

 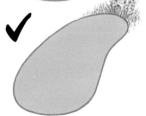

Spring bulbs in flower are always a welcome sight but they should not be planted in a luxury or utility lawn. The grass cannot be cut for 6 weeks after the blooms have faded, so naturalise Narcissi etc in rough grassland.

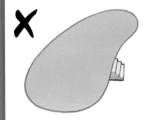 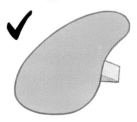

Avoid restricted access to the lawn. If there is just one narrow entry point then excessive wear and bare patches are inevitable, and that means some reseeding or returfing. Make sure that the mower can be moved easily on and off the lawn.

Viola types

PANSIES

V. 'Padparadja'
Plain type

V. 'Joker'
Faced type

V. 'Rippling Waters'
Bicoloured type

VIOLAS

V. 'Johnny Jump-up'

V. 'Chantreyland'

BORDER VIOLETS

V. cornuta

Name that shrub

Medium or large shrub
•
Deciduous
or
Evergreen
•
Colour available

•
Flowering period

| JANUARY |
| FEBRUARY |
| MARCH |
| APRIL |
| MAY |
| JUNE |
| —— JULY —— |
| AUGUST |
| SEPTEMBER |
| OCTOBER |
| NOVEMBER |
| DECEMBER |

One of the showiest specimen shrubs available, but not often seen in gardens. There are a couple of problems. The most popular ones are large shrubs which become tree-like in time, and so shortage of space rules it out for many gardeners. The other problem is that it is not easy to grow, requiring shelter and a fertile, well-drained site. Begin with a container-grown specimen and plant it close to a wall to protect it from strong winds. Grow ground cover plants around the base of the newly-planted shrub. Your reward will be a stunning display of large white blooms.

Answer on page 128

Pruning evergreens

Only a few evergreens need cutting back every year as a matter of routine. Erica, Calluna and Lavandula should be lightly trimmed as soon as the flowers have faded. Grey-leaved ground-cover evergreens such as Artemisia, Senecio and Santolina, as well as Vinca and Pachysandra, should be trimmed in early spring.

When to Prune

With nearly all evergreens, spring is the best season and March is the best month. Where winter-damaged branches are to be removed it is best to wait until late spring to see the full extent of the damage and to see if there has been any regrowth. With spring-flowering evergreen shrubs prune as soon as the blooms have faded. The worst time for pruning evergreens is August-October.

Rose types

Hybrid Tea

The classic Rose – a pointed bud opening into a many-petalled flower with a high central cone. But it is not the ideal Rose – many Hybrid Tea bushes are upright and rigid, and the blooms of many varieties are ruined by heavy rain. In general they flower less frequently and provide less colour than Floribundas. New varieties appear every year – check the catalogues and pick ones with good disease resistance.

Floribunda

The typical Floribunda produces blooms which lack the size, beauty and fragrance of their more elegant rival – the Hybrid Tea Rose. But there are advantages – these bushes provide a larger splash of colour and have a longer flowering season. The average Floribunda is also hardier, easier to care for and more reliable in wet weather than its Hybrid Tea counterpart. Follow the modern way to prune on page 115.

Patio

These dwarf Floribunda Roses have become increasingly popular for planting at the front of the border and in containers. When grown in pots you must make sure that they are watered regularly in dry weather, and in early spring the bushes should be pruned in the same way as their larger relatives – see page 115. Make sure you choose a variety which claims good disease resistance in the catalogue or on the label.

Miniature

These tiny-leaved plants are smaller than Patio Roses, and are generally grown in pots to provide a colourful season-long display. Maintenance is not quite as easy as some people think. Pruning is straightforward (see page 115), but pests and diseases can be a problem. Regular watering in dry weather is essential, and the fairy-like form may disappear in time. Plant pot-grown specimens in spring.

Shrub

This class is a wide-ranging rag-bag of varieties. There are tiny ones and giants, types which bloom for a few short weeks and others which are in flower all season long. Some, such as the Rugosas, are extremely easy to grow as they are remarkably resistant to disease – there are others which have little or no resistance. The rule is to check the label and/or catalogue description carefully before buying.

Climber

There are two types of climbing Roses. Ramblers have long pliable stems with large flower trusses. There is generally only one flush, and they are not a good choice for the green gardener. They have little resistance to mildew and the need for regular pruning is a chore. Climbers are a better choice. Larger flowers are borne on stiffer stems which provide a permanent framework – maintenance and pruning are easier.

Ground Cover

Shrub Roses with a distinctly spreading or trailing growth habit have been moved to a class of their own – the Ground Cover Roses. The leafy mounds are useful for covering banks or manhole covers, but nearly all varieties can grow to 60 cm or more when mature. There are a few which reach only 45 cm or less.

The four basic growth types are ground cover, bush, standard and climbing (see chart below). A bush may be a Hybrid Tea, Patio, Miniature, Floribunda or Shrub Rose.

Prostrate Rose	Miniature Bush	Miniature Standard	Dwarf Bush	Bush	Half Standard	Full Standard	Weeping Standard	Pillar Rose	Climbing Rose
30 cm or less	40 cm or less	stem 40 cm	60 cm or less	over 60 cm	stem 75 cm	stem 1 m	stem 1.5 m	approx 2.5 m	

House plant design terms

SCALE

Scale is the relationship of the plant and its container to the size and shape of the room and its furniture — the aim is to ensure that they are in proportion. A tall and spreading palm in a small hall can look hopelessly out of place, whereas a scatter of isolated pots of small plants would spoil the appearance of a large room decorated in a contemporary style.

There are no rules to show how to ensure that the scale is right, but there are guidelines. A floor-standing tree-like plant is the best choice if you are dealing with a large, bare area. Do think big — an average-sized plant may well look lost. A specimen with wide-spreading or drooping leaves will appear to lower the ceiling — a tall, column-like plant will seem to add height to the ceiling.

Don't buy a specimen tree on impulse. Measure the height and width you want to cover before you leave the room, and then take your tape measure to the garden centre to find a plant which will fit the bill.

Rogues gallery

Potato

Tomato

POTATO BLIGHT

The first signs are brown patches on potato or tomato leaves — in damp weather each blight spot on the underside has a fringe of white mould. This disease can destroy all the foliage in a wet season. The disease does not travel down the stems to the tubers — the fungal spores are washed off the leaves and on to the soil by rain. If the tubers come into contact with live spores when harvesting then the tubers will develop blight in store. To prevent this from happening earth up the stems to keep the tubers covered and then cut off and remove all diseased growth 10 days before lifting. Infected tomatoes develop brown, sunken areas and soon rot. It is necessary to treat a potato crop with a fungicide at regular intervals if you want to prevent this disease. Spray potato plants with a copper-based spray in July — treat tomatoes as soon as they have been stopped. Repeat every 2 weeks if the weather is damp.

Lm 5/10

Answers

Name that flower	Name that shrub

Name that flower

page
- 13 Nigella (Love-in-a-mist)
- 37 Chionodoxa (Glory of the snow)
- 52 Amaranthus (Love-lies-bleeding)
- 82 Gazania (Gazania)
- 85 Portulaca (Sun Plant)
- 101 Echium (Annual Borage)
- 118 Alstroemeria (Peruvian Lily)

Name that shrub

page
- 8 Choisya (Mexican Orange Blossom)
- 24 Romneya (Tree Poppy)
- 41 Callicarpa (Beauty Berry)
- 57 Fremontodendron (Flannel Flower)
- 69 Pernettya (Prickly Heath)
- 85 Sarcococca (Christmas Box)
- 111 Genista (Broom)
- 125 Eucryphia (Brush Bush)

Acknowledgements

It would be quite impossible to acknowledge all of the people who have helped to create the Experts over the past 50 years. Sadly, the small group who were involved with me right at the beginning are no longer with us — artist Henry Barber, designer John Woodbridge, Denis Nahum and my dear wife Joan.

In the middle period there were many others, some helping with a book or two and a few people, such as John Adkins and Paul Norris of pbi Publications, who were part of the team for many years.

And so on to today, with this Expert and the ones to come. Where do we start? In the kitchen, I suppose, where all the ingredients are put together. Photographs from Garden Picture Library, artworks from Christine Wilson, proof-reading by Angelina Gibbs, repro skills from Barry Highland and Ian Harris, and finally my long serving (and long suffering) Girl Friday Gill Jackson.

This book, however, would be in a storeroom somewhere if it was not for the marketing and sales efforts of the people at Transworld Publishers — notably M.D. Larry Finlay, Gareth Pottle, Martin Higgins, Ed Christie, Janine Giovanni and Claire Evans.

To all these people and many more, past and present, I owe a great debt of gratitude. And also to my father, who gave me my first packet of seeds.